Illustrated

DODGE
PICKUP
BUYER'S ★ GUIDE™

Don Bunn

Motorbooks International
Publishers & Wholesalers

First published in 1994 by Motorbooks International Publishers & Wholesalers, PO Box 2, 729 Prospect Avenue, Osceola, WI 54020 USA

Motorbooks International books are also available at discounts in bulk quantity for industrial or sales-promotional use. For details write to Special Sales Manager at the Publisher's address

Library of Congress Cataloging-in-Publication Data
    Bunn, Don.
        Illustrated Dodge pickup buyer's guide/ Don Bunn.
            p. cm. — (Motorbooks International illustrated buyer's guide series)
        Includes index.
    ISBN 0-87938-847-1
    1. Dodge trucks—Purchasing. 2. Dodge trucks —Collectors and collecting. 3. Dodge trucks —History. I. Title. II. Series.
    TL230.5.D63B763   1994
    629.223—dc20 93-32131

On the front cover: The past and the look of the future come together in this photo of a 1938 RC half-ton pickup owned by Bill Dyer, Lakeland, Florida, and a 1994 Ram 1500, courtesy of Dodge Division, Chrysler Corporation. *Mike Mueller*

Printed and bound in the United States of America

Contents

Acknowledgments

It would have been impossible to write this book without the assistance of a number of willing and knowledgeable friends, for one cannot write a comprehensive, interesting, and accurate work without their input. It is my pleasure to acknowledge the assistance of the following people who made this volume possible. They generously gave of their time and talents.

First I'd like to thank Joel Miller of Portland, Oregon, who wrote the chapter on "Vans and Small Trucks," the "Adult Toys" and "Sport Utility" sidebars, and gave valuable input to the balance of the book by proofreading and advising on the entire manuscript.

Special thanks to Jim Benjaminson, who wrote the chapter on "Plymouth Commercials." Jim is "Mr. Plymouth," the most qualified person to write the Plymouth chapter. Jim's book, *Plymouth 1946-1959*, published by Motorbooks International, should be in every Chrysler lover's library.

I'd also like to give special recognition to Herb Von Rusten. Herb recently retired from Chrysler after forty years in Dodge truck engineering. Herb provided many valuable insights that otherwise would never have been known. He is one of the key men who engineered our favorite trucks from 1951 to 1992.

Another longtime friend who contributed in a major way is artist Greg Norman of Richfield, Minnesota, who drew the excellent illustrations. Greg was also available for counsel whenever I needed him.

My Canadian friend Carl Friberg authored the "Slant-Six" sidebar. Carl is first and foremost an In-ternational Harvester expert, but Carl also appreciates Chrysler's unique slant six engine and the vehicles it powered.

Most of the photos are courtesy of Chrysler Corporation, and some are from the author's collection, or as noted from individual truck owners. Special thanks to the many Dodge collectors who provided photos of their trucks.

Others whose contributions I value highly are:

Dinah Bunn, Bloomington, Minnesota; Robert Bunn, Bloomington, Minnesota; Roy Smith, Detroit, Michigan; Bruce Welle, Sauk Centre, Minnesota; Steve Fish, Bloomington, Minnesota; Tom Brownell, Big Rapids, Michigan; Dick Copello, York, Pennsylvania; Jerry Bougher, Albany, Oregon; Elliott Kahn, Clearwater Beach, Florida; Todd Erdman, Lakeville, Minnesota; John Zentmyer, Los Angeles, California; George Rabuse, St Paul, Minnesota; Paul McLaughlin, Albuquerque, New Mexico; Manfred Strobel, Orchard Lake, Michigan; Paul Kleppert, Detroit, Michigan; Jim Wren, Detroit, Michigan; Dan Kirchner, Dearborn, Michigan; Ron Cenowa, Utica, Michigan; Don Lawrence, Fargo, North Dakota; Greg Tomberlin, Brainerd, Minnesota; Tom Berndt, Rogers, Minnesota; and Tom Gale, Detroit, Michigan.

I invite anyone who has something to share about Dodge trucks to feel free to write or call: 5109 West 105th Street, Bloomington, MN 55437, 612-831-2309.

Don Bunn
January 1994

Introduction

Maxwell, the "Triumvirate" Dodge Brothers, Graham Brothers, and Chrysler People

Recounting the history of Dodge trucks is a bit more complicated than merely remembering the efforts of a single marque. Actually, three separate roots sprang up and twisted together to form the giant Chrysler Corporation.

The Maxwell Company

The roots of Chrysler-built trucks can be traced all the way back to the Maxwell Motor Company, a Detroit automobile manufacturer founded in 1905. In addition to making cars, Maxwell also built light trucks. Its first truck came onto the market in 1917, a one-tonner powered by Maxwell's four-cylinder engine. A light-duty delivery truck was new in 1918. It was built on the Maxwell Four passenger car's chassis and was powered by its four-cylinder engine. This truck was built in an effort to maximize the return on existing components and production facilities. The light delivery truck lasted until 1925.

Walter Chrysler became involved with debt-ridden Maxwell in 1921. Maxwell was in very poor shape and was plagued by a negative reputation because of past quality problems. Maxwell's Four wasn't very well accepted in the marketplace because it was an old, tired design dating back to the mid-teens.

From the time he became involved with Maxwell, Walter Chrysler was determined to build a car with his name on it. He moved his engineering brain trust, the "Triumvirate" (Fred M. Zeder, Owen Skelton, and Carl Breer), into the old Chalmers plant in Detroit. They designed an all-new light car with a high-performance six-cylinder engine. Walter named it the Chrysler Six and put it on the market in 1924. Even though it was named the Chrysler Six, it was a model of the Maxwell Motor Company. Walter Chrysler had realized his dream—a quality, high-performance, trend-setting car bearing his name. The Chrysler Six was an immediate success, outselling by far the Maxwell Four.

Before Walter Chrysler bought Dodge Brothers in July 1928, this ad (from *The Country Gentleman*, May 1928) was one of the last Graham Brothers truck ads. After the Chrysler buy-out, all Graham Brothers trucks were renamed Dodge Brothers. Note the ad reads, "Built by truck division of the Dodge Brothers, Inc." The one-ton G-Boy pickup is shown. *Jerry Bougher*

5

In 1925 Chrysler figured it was time to straighten out the corporate structure because—after only four years—he had repaid Maxwell's debts and had $5 million in the bank. This he did by changing the corporation's name to the Chrysler Corporation, and consequently Maxwell Motors ceased to be.

Chrysler's Engineering "Triumvirate"

Chrysler Corporation's engineering excellence began even before the Chrysler Corporation was formed. The "Triumvirate," as they were called in the early years, of Zeder, Skelton, and Breer, worked together for many years before joining the Chrysler Corp. Zeder, their leader, became associated with Walter Chrysler in 1920 at Willys. Walter Chrysler had been hired by this troubled company's (Willys) bankers to turn it around. Zeder left Willys in 1922 to become president of his newly formed firm of engineering consultants, the Zeder, Skelton, and Breer Engineering Corporation.

Walter Chrysler hired them in 1923 at Maxwell Motors. In less than a year they completed development work on the new Chrysler car and had it in production. When the Chrysler Corporation was formed, they dissolved their engineering company and went on Chrysler's payroll.

Zeder became vice president in charge of engineering and was known as the engineering genius behind every Chrysler-built vehicle. The other two became executive engineers. Skelton was the designer of the trio, while Breer's speciality was engineering research and experimental work. Zeder set up a central engineering department that controlled all corporate engineering. However, each operating unit had its own engineering department that worked with central engineering.

Dodge Brothers

In another part of the bustling, vibrant city of Detroit, two brothers named Dodge—Horace and John—were becoming firmly established as a manufacturer of high-quality, medium-priced cars and trucks.

These two master engineers got their start in business making bicycles in the late 1800s. With the rise of the auto business, they shifted gears and began building high-quality components. Their first big car parts customer was Ransom Olds. In 1901 the Dodges built transmissions for the historic curved-dash Oldsmobile. A few years later, they hooked up with the ambitious Henry Ford. Dodge built everything for Ford's Model T except its body, wheels, and tires. Business was good, and both parties prospered greatly.

Henry finally reached the point where he wanted all the action for himself, so he began to vertically integrate his manufacturing empire. The brothers Dodge saw the handwriting on the wall and determined to develop a car of their own. They knew better than to try to out-Model T the Model T, so instead they pegged their car up-market from the T in size, price, and quality. Using the money realized from the dividends, profits, and stock sale from their relationship with Mr. Ford, they had their first Dodge car on the road late in 1914.

In the early years truck building was about the last thing John and Horace wanted to get into, because the factory couldn't even build enough cars to satisfy demand. The Dodge Brothers Company enjoyed a reputation for quality even before they built their first car. However, their customers, through their dealers, were pushing the factory hard for a Dodge truck. They wanted a truck as tough and dependable as Dodge cars. The pressure to add trucks to the line became stronger with the passage of time and as more Dodge cars were sold.

The US Army and World War I pushed Dodge over the edge. There was no way the brothers were going to back away from their duty to support America in the war effort. They did so, by the way, by also mass producing a 155-millimeter howitzer, a feat many said was impossible. (See chapters one and ten for details of Dodge trucks in World War I.)

Tragically, in 1920 both John and Horace Dodge died in the prime of their lives. Their company was purchased by an investment banking company that continued to run it in somewhat the manner the brothers would have approved of. The company continued to prosper greatly.

Graham Brothers

The three Graham brothers of Indiana—Joseph, Robert, and Ray—began their business careers in the glass blowing business. When that business was sold, they turned their attention to truck building. In the beginning they built kits that converted a car chassis into a truck. They also converted auto chassis, built by a number of companies, into light- and medium-duty trucks.

In 1921 Graham Brothers closed a deal with Dodge in which they would use the Dodge-built chassis exclusively and then sell their Graham Brothers trucks only through the vast Dodge Brothers dealer network. This business arrangement worked like a charm. In 1921 Graham Brothers built only ton-and-a-half trucks and buses. It was not long until their line expanded to include everything from half-ton to two-and-a-half-ton trucks and buses. The Dodge four-cylinder engine powered all Graham Brothers trucks until 1928, when the first six-cylinder-powered truck was completed. Graham Brothers built their own bodies in company-owned factories.

In 1927 Dodge bought Graham Brothers, and the truck building division of Dodge Brothers became a wholly owned division. The Graham brothers left to start their own automobile company. Walter Chrysler wanted desperately to acquire Dodge because Dodge was a very tough competitor. He also needed Dodge's extensive dealer network. The huge Hamtramck complex with its foundry was the production complex Chrysler needed to expand his auto empire. In 1928 he bought Dodge, including Graham Brothers, and began building Plymouth and DeSoto cars. Consequently, Walter Chrysler instantly became a major force in US car and truck building. It was also in August 1928 when Chrysler's new Fargo Division began building trucks.

There you have it. All three roots were pulled together in 1928 to become the Chrysler Corporation that we now know. There is, of course, a fourth root—Jeep, but Jeep will be outside the scope of this book.

Chrysler People

To say the story of Chrysler-built trucks was limited to a handful of successful, well-to-do businessmen would be a travesty. The fact of the matter is that many thousands of men and women over the years were responsible for building the trucks we know, own, and love. The people who designed, engineered, built, and sold them included workers in offices, plants, stores, and studios. They were white collar and blue collar workers, union members and management. They included men like Herb Von Rusten, now retired, who for forty years was a creative, hard-working Dodge truck engineer. Roy Smith, another engineer, is the plant manager at Dodge City. Roy directs the thousands of employees at that huge complex in building full-size Ram and midsize Dakota pickups.

Top executives like Tom Gale, vice president of product design, also contributed. Gale is a twenty-five-year Chrysler veteran and has been in

In 1941 Plymouth built both cars and trucks for America's farmers. This last Plymouth commercial pick-up was a rugged truck-built half-ton and was well suited to strenuous farm work. This ad appeared in *The Prairie Farmer* (January 11, 1941). *Jerry Bougher*

From the end of World War II to the late fifties, Dodge Truck's advertising featured a number of full-color original works of art in its ads. A one-ton pickup is pictured in this ad from *Life* magazine (March 18, 1946). *Stephen March*

charge of Chrysler's design studios since 1985. Tom and his design team are responsible for creating the world-class 1994 T300 full-size Dodge Ram pickup and award-winning Chrysler cars and Jeeps.

One important quality that contributes mightily to his success and to the success of Robert Lutz, Chrysler's president, is that both of these dynamic executives are dyed-in-the-wool "car people," not financial wizards. And it shows in Chrysler's product lineup. Who but a real "car guy" would have taken the time to find a 1954 Power Wagon and then talk the company into buying it, as Tom Gale recently did? It is my hope that in the following pages you will find the right Dodge truck to suit your style, needs, and pocketbook. Thankfully, we all have our own unique interests and reasons for the vintage Dodge truck that is correct for us. There is a Dodge out there to suit everyone.

Investment Ratings

The five-star rating system is a general collector or user rating as follows:

★ Models in abundant supply that have slow upward appreciation. Prices may be low, although fine examples may command higher prices if for no other reason than that they provide good transportation. These trucks offer a good and inexpensive entry into the hobby.

★★ Models that have found substantial collector interest and are being bought and have a good chance for future appreciation. Unrestored examples may still be bargains.

★★★ Models that have had greater appreciation and are targeted by collectors.

★★★★ Models that are rare and highly regarded by all truck enthusiasts.

★★★★★ Particular models of exceptional interest and rarity that have realized their highest values and have strong collector markets.

Chapter 1

Pioneer Trucks 1916-1932

★★★	1916-1918 Dodge chassis with aftermarket commercial bodies
★★★★	1920-1928 Graham trucks
★★★★★	1918-1928 Dodge Commercial screensides and panels
★★★★★	1924-1932 Dodge Commercial pickups

I am indebted to Don Butler, lately of Detroit, for details of the vehicles built by the original Dodge Brothers Company. Don began writing after retiring from the Chrysler Corporation, where he had worked for many years as a stylist. He is best known for his expertly written, thoroughly researched, and comprehensive book, *The Plymouth-DeSoto Story.* Don also wrote a series of articles for *Cars & Parts* magazine on the four-cylinder automobiles built by the original Dodge Brothers Company between 1914 and 1928. Most of the source material Don used was from personal notes kept by a Dodge Brothers worker who was employed from 1914 until the thirties. This anonymous factory worker made notes on all the changes he observed as they were incorporated into Dodge vehicles as they moved down the assembly line at Dodge Main in Hamtramck, Michigan. He worked at a job where he could observe all the changes and activities in the plant.

This 1918 Dodge Brothers car was converted to a pickup by removing its back seat and replacing it with a homemade cargo box. Conversions of this type were common in the Pioneer Era.

This 1919 Maxwell pickup was a forefather of all Chrysler Corporation-built trucks. Walter Chrysler parlayed Maxwell Motors Company into the Chrysler Corporation in 1925. *S. T. Moody*

The First Dodge Commercials

Dodge's first passenger car was completed on November 14, 1914, but was considered a 1915 model year vehicle. One year and one day later, on November 15, 1915, the first commercial chassis (which was actually a beefed-up car chassis) moved down the assembly line. This chassis was shipped out to have a body installed by an outside manufacturer.

Another historic event occurred on August 31, 1916. The first Dodge Brothers chassis, which had been engineered as a commercial chassis, was completed. This could have been the first of many chassis units Dodge built and shipped to its distributor in England.

In 1920 Dodge Brother's screenside was in its third year of production. Its appearance was unchanged from 1918. This truck has a payload capacity of 1,000lb, hence the half-ton rating. *Robert Quirk*

World War I Trucks

Don's article is surprisingly silent concerning the trucks and chassis units Dodge built for the US Army either before or during World War I, but certainly this first commercial chassis engineered by Dodge for commercial work was also the chassis unit Dodge supplied to others for mounting of special war-use bodies. Dodge dealers from the very earliest days pressured the factory for a light-duty commercial to sell. Dodge management was hard to convince, because they couldn't build all the cars their dealers could sell.

The US Army purchased its first Dodge automobiles late in 1915. Less than two years after the first Dodge cars were built, an event took place that established early Dodge cars in the minds of Americans as the car that could be depended upon when the going was tough. Six US Army 1916 Dodge tourings with soft tops starred in a skirmish called the 1916 Punitive Expedition against the Mexican bandit leader Pancho Villa. These Dodges were the first automobiles ever to be used in an American military action against an armed enemy. We are not talking four-wheel-drive, special tires, low silhouette, winch, and armor here, but just an off-the-line touring with nothing more than a coat of olive drab paint. The soldiers depended on the Dodge's superior speed and toughness to get the job done. Villa and his bandits had conducted a number of raids across the border into New Mexico. Brigadier General John J. "Black Jack" Pershing, the commander of the US Army Force, and his staff rode in three 1916 Dodge tourings. The Dodges proved their dependability when a reporter with the Pershing Expedition wrote: "Over the desert stretch, and by nature of the desert dust, three camouflaged automobiles swayed and lurched and banged in low gear, belching steam from their radiators, grinding their way through the sand. Tanks would have been better suited to the journey."

Lt. George S. Patton

A second incident in this same effort against the Mexicans firmly and forever established Dodge as *the* dependable one and in the process made military history. Lt. George S. Patton Jr. led the first mechanized cavalry charge in the US Army's history, with three dependable Dodges. In exasperation, when his cavalry failed in an effort to round up a group of bandits near Chihuahua, Mexico, Patton decided to switch to three Dodge tourings for their superior speed. George Patton's "Chargers," or Dodge "War Wagons," each carried five fully armed soldiers into battle. Now you know where the names Dodge Charger and Ramcharger come from. The Dodges proved worthy of accomplishing a job at which the Army's cavalry failed.

"We couldn't have done it with horses. The motor car is the modern war horse," said Lt. Patton in a *Motor Age* article. The article went on to say, "There are no roads worthy of the name. The cars have to be driven through sand, or loose rock, up and down grades and even across mountain streams. The staff cars stand up remarkably well, though there has naturally been a little trouble with springs. General Pershing has ordered that only Dodges be used by his staff."

The six original Army Dodge tourings performed so well in combat that General Pershing requested 250 more by July 15, 1916, as reported in the July 16, 1916, issue of *Automobile Topics* magazine.

World War I

Very soon after the Mexican skirmish ended, the United States found itself involved in Europe in World War I. The war against Germany started at 1:18 p.m. Eastern Time on April 6, 1917, when President Wilson signed a declaration of war. The details of Dodge's participation in World War I are, unfortunately, cloudy. We do not know for sure exactly what types of trucks or what quantities were employed in France by the A.E.F. (American Expeditionary Forces). One reason for the confusion is that the government's procurement practices and records in those days were inadequate, to say the least. Another important reason for the confusion stems from the fact that in the early years of motor car development the common practice was for automakers to provide chassis and cabs on which others would mount bodies of all types.

These vehicles were called "commercial cars"—the equivalent of today's half-ton trucks. We know that the Army purchased many Dodge chassis onto which they applied several different bodies. Two of these were the light repair truck (a pickup box with canvas cover) and an ambulance. Both were used in large quantities. The Army also purchased delivery box, transport body, and rolling kitchen bodies, according to records kept by the Budd Co., which supplied the bodies. It is estimated that between 1916 and the end of World War I, the government purchased a total of between 15,000-20,000 Dodge vehicles of all types.

The Army vehicle purchased in the largest quantities from Dodge was the screenside. We know this from an article in the November 24, 1917, issue of *Automobile Topics*, which announced the arrival of the screenside to the commercial market. The article said, "It is stated that a large number of commercial cars, of which the new model (a screenside was pictured) is practically a duplicate, have been delivered by Dodge Brothers to the government each month for several months."

A 1924 Graham Brothers one-ton stake truck. Graham Brothers built trucks on Dodge Brother's chassis with Dodge's dependable four-cylinder engines. Graham Brothers built truck bodies in their own plants. Dodge Brothers and Graham Brothers are the other forefathers of Chrysler-built trucks. *Jack Murray*

This 1924 Dodge Brothers screenside was found in St Paul, Minnesota. Front bumpers were an extra-cost option in 1924; that's why it's not uncommon to find trucks of this vintage without them.

By the time World War I ended, Dodge's performance as a tough, dependable war machine had become solidly established with auto owners from coast to coast. Dodge was the car and commercial car with dependability. Dodge owners who knew this dependability firsthand put the new word "dependability" in the dictionary.

Early Civilian Trucks

Let's shift gears from military trucks now into civilian trucks. It is rather interesting that the first US-built Dodge commercial car was exactly the same screenside the Army purchased. I suspect this was more than a matter of mere coincidence. In any event, Dodge's first commercial car was built on a passenger car's 114in wheelbase chassis, but the commercial's frame was longer, and it was built with many heavy-duty components such as heavier springs to allow the commercial to carry its maximum load safely. The commercial was finished in the same quality black enamel paint as used on the Dodge cars. The 15 gallon (gal) fuel tank fitted with a fuel gauge was located under the driver's seat and fed fuel to the carburetor by gravity. In the Dodge passenger car, the fuel tank was located in the cowl. Another departure from the car was in the fact that the commercial's steering column and wheel were set at a higher angle. Front springs were semielliptic, and the rear springs were three-quarter elliptic. The body's loading space was 72in long by 43in wide, and 54in high

from floor to top inside. It had plain-tread front tires and nonskid tread on the rears. Wheels were sturdily built from twelve hickory spokes, front and rear, with a side-mounted spare. Tires were 33x4 all around. The windshield was of the opening (or as they called them in those days, ventilating) type. Headlights and taillights were electric.

Standard Equipment

Standard equipment included an electric horn, license brackets, tire pump, jack, tool kit, and a side-mounted tire carrier with demountable rim located on the side of the body just behind the driver's door. The instrument panel was well equipped with a 60mph speedometer; a total and trip mileage recorder; oil pressure gauge; a locking ignition and lighting switch; an ammeter; choke; and an instrument panel light. This first Dodge commercial topped the scales at 2,610lb and was rated at 1,000lb carrying capacity, or half-ton. The first Dodge commercial car boasted an all-steel body built by the Budd Co.

Dodge in these early days always began the new model year on July 1 and ended it on June 30, so the first commercial was in fact a 1918 model year vehicle. It was priced at $885. The seat was upholstered in genuine leather, by the way.

An interesting historical note is that while this first commercial was called a screenside, it was equipped with both screens and side curtains (canopy sides) for the sides and rear, which were

A 1924 Dodge Brothers commercial panel. These small trucks were equipped with rear brakes only. *Applegate and Applegate*

of oiled duck. A few years later it was the common practice to differentiate between a screen and a canopy. The screen was on the base vehicle, and side curtains were an added-cost option. We are not talking about two distinct and separate models, but rather the same truck equipped one way or the

The Story of Fargo Trucks

Long before its purchase of Dodge Brothers, Chrysler management had decided to organize a new and separate company, the Fargo Motor Corporation, through which Chrysler would build and market commercial vehicles. Production began on the first Fargo—called the Clipper, Series-ED—in August 1928. It had a three-quarter-ton chassis with cowl. In September, 1928, the Packet 4 Series-EE, a half-ton chassis with cowl, was added. The half-ton was priced at $545 list, and the three-quarter-ton was priced at $725. One of two bodies could be added to either chassis-cowl: a Panel at $250 or a Glass Side at $725. The Panel body was designed for commercial delivery work, while the Glass Side, at $350, was a dual-purpose vehicle designed for delivery and/or passenger use. One option for the Glass Side was a "full-width crosswise seat"; by adding seats, the owner could create a large station wagon to haul people or cargo.

Let me make it clear that these first Fargo trucks, built from 1928-1930, were "Chrysler" trucks and not "Dodge" trucks. They were designed and engineered by Chrysler before its purchase of Dodge and did not share any parts with the Dodge trucks of 1928. In fact, these first Fargos were built with components from the Chrysler 65, DeSoto, and Plymouth passenger cars. Bodies for the Panel and Glass Side were purchased from outside body manufacturers.

A new series of Packet half-ton and Clipper three-quarter-ton, six-cylinder trucks was introduced in March 1929, and the one-ton Freighter was added in June. Body choices expanded greatly with the addition of canopy, screen, sedan, pickup, platform, stake, farm box, and stock rack. These many additional bodies show the influence of Chrysler's purchase of Dodge Brothers. The Dodge Brothers Division built these bodies in their own plants, making it a simple matter to mount them onto Fargo chassis. Fargo trucks continued more-or-less unchanged until production ceased in November 1930. Production total for all years, all models, is estimated at 9,670 trucks, of which only thirty-nine were built in Canada, the rest in Detroit.

Fargo also built buses from 1930-1932, including school buses (separate and distinct from a Dodge truck chassis fitted with an aftermarket school bus body), Street Car Coaches, and Parlor Cars. These 165in-238in wheelbase buses were big, over-the-road rigs powered by huge straight-eight L-head engines, although some smaller units were powered by sixes. Their styling, chassis, and bodies were unlike anything in the Dodge truck line; the only items common to both were engines and transmissions. Total production was small, and based on serial numbers, I estimate it at approximately 235. Fargo buses were sold directly to operators because buses were presumed to be fleet sales vehicles and outside the sales realm of the typical Dodge dealer.

Starting in 1933, US-made Fargo trucks were exported throughout the world, but were not sold in Mexico. Canadian production of Fargos began in 1936; they were sold exclusively in Canada. DeSoto trucks, built in the US only, were exported to Mexico, as well as to other parts of the world. For some unexplained reason the word *Fargo* was not accepted in Mexico.

In the early thirties, Chrysler's marketing was very different in Canada than in the US. In the States, each division stood alone, while in Canada, since the market was smaller, Chrysler and Plymouth were paired, as were DeSoto and Dodge. Chrysler-Plymouth consequently had no truck to sell. Chrysler solved this problem by giving Chrysler-Plymouth dealers the Fargo truck line in 1936. At first, Fargo built only half-ton, ton-and-a-half, and two-ton trucks, but by 1939 the line-up included trucks all the way up to four tons.

Fargo trucks after 1933 were rebadged Dodges; however, there were some differences, notably in front-end sheetmetal, nameplates, and ornamentation. And in the forties and fifties, the Canadian plants used only the large-block L-six for all trucks up to two tons. By decreasing its bore and stroke, overall displacement was about equivalent to US-produced light-duty Dodge trucks. Other than these differences, Fargos were, for all intents and purposes, the same vehicles as Dodges. The careful observer will note that with the passage of time, distinctions between the two became fewer and fewer. Fargo trucks are still produced in various parts of the world (Turkey, for example), even though the Fargo nameplate was discontinued in Canada in 1972.

In 1924 screensides were a favored work truck with tradesmen. They were a cross between a pickup and a panel.

other, or with both, depending upon the owner's preference. The oiled duck side curtains easily rolled up and then tied at the top of the side openings when not needed.

A report on this new Dodge commercial in the November 24, 1917, issue of *Automobile Topics* makes this interesting statement: "It is precisely the kind of light delivery car that one would expect the Dodge Brothers to build." In other words, the author said that the commercial is the same fine quality vehicle as the Dodge Brothers passenger cars

A gorgeous 1926 Dodge Brothers commercial screenside. Note the absence of extra-cost front bumper. *S. T. Moody*

that were now in their fourth model year. According to James Wren in his excellent book, *Motor Trucks of America*, the screenside was introduced at the Boston Automobile Show, March 3-10, 1917. The screenside for civilian use went into production beginning in August 1917, at which time seventy-seven units were built; by the end of the calendar year, a total of 720 units had been assembled. So as soon as the factory learned how to handle production of the screenside, that first trickle quickly became a torrent.

Panel Model

The first fully enclosed panel commercial car was built five months later, on March 26, 1918, but was still considered a 1918 model. Its chassis details were exactly the same as for the screenside. It sold for $935. By the way, the terms *business car* and *commercial* were used interchangeably for either the screenside or panel. The panel was built with closed sides and with two rear full-height cargo doors with glass windows. The Army purchased a small quantity of these same panels.

Dodge's First Panel

This was not the first panel in Dodge's short history. Just over one year earlier on November 19, 1916, the British magazine *Motor Traction* carried an article called "A New Dodge Light Delivery Van." Dodge shipped chassis cowls to its representative in the United Kindom—Charles Jarrott and

Letts, Ltd., who built a smart-looking panel body (not the same as the US-built panel) in England and mounted it on the imported Dodge chassis. No mention was made of a screenside. Is the screenside a unique American truck? Maybe so, as it was the forerunner of our all-American pickup. After all, a screenside is really a pickup with a roof and available canvas covers to close it weathertight.

The Last of the Dodge Brothers Trucks

These two commercial cars—the screenside and the panel—stayed in production from late 1917 until 1926 (August 29, 1926, for the panel and September 5, 1926, for the screenside). They changed little over the years except for the styling and engineering updates also made to the Dodge cars. They went out of production in 1926 because late in 1925 Dodge Brothers Inc. bought out Graham Brothers Inc., and the Graham brothers retired from the company. At this time all trucks built by the Dodge Brothers Co. were badged as Graham Brothers. Up to this point, the Graham Brothers Division was only involved with trucks, one-ton and heavier. But now the Graham Brothers Division took over the responsibility for commercial cars, too. Beginning in 1925, for those customers who hauled bulky but light loads, Dodge began to build a 96in panel on a 140in-wheelbase chassis. These 8ft panels were produced by Dodge only in 1925 and 1926.

While maintaining the same engine and transmission without change except for those noted below, the two commercial cars—screenside and panel—soldiered on with but minor changes up to 1928, at which time the original Dodge Brothers Company was purchased by an ambitious Walter Chrysler who was eager to expand his growing auto empire. In order to modernize these two commercials over time to make them better suited to carry out their intended tasks, these major updates were made (in chronological order):

1. 1923: The radiator was raised by 3.5in, and, by necessity, the cowl and hood were also raised the same amount. This simple change contributed mightily to improving their appearance; the new look was one of a more heavy-duty truck.

2. 1924: Wheelbase was stretched to 116in. With the longer wheelbase came the upgrade to a three-quarter-ton capacity. The cargo box was increased to 72.5in long by 44in wide and 50.25in high, giving a load area of 84cu-ft. In order to better support this load-carrying capacity, rear springs were lengthened to 55in, but were now of the half-elliptic type and underslung. For better engine cooling, hood louvers were provided.

3. 1925: This was the first year for a fully enclosed cab with roll-up glass windows in cab doors and a seat like a passenger car; a welcome improvement for drivers who lived in cold climates. On August 28, 1925, the conventional gear shift pattern was adopted for commercials only. Also this year, a 140in-wheelbase chassis was engineered for the Graham Brothers on which a 96in panel body could be mounted. These were only built in limited quantities for those who wanted to

This 1929 Dodge ton-and-a-half pickup's styling was heavily influenced by Graham Brothers. 1929 was the first model year Dodge Truck Division was owned by Chrysler. *Paul McLaughlin*

By 1930 Dodge truck's styling was heavily influenced by Chrysler Corporation, as seen by this 1931 commercial screenside. *Ron Cenowa*

haul bulky but light loads. The spare tire mounting was moved to be underslung at the rear.

4. 1926: Commercial cars were given the new engine with five main bearings, a change made in the passenger cars three months earlier. This change did not increase the engine's output or cubic inch displacement (cid).

On October 4, 1926, the last commercial panel was built in Dodge Main Plant No. One. All commercial car production was shifted out to the Graham Brothers plants in Detroit, Michigan; Evansville, Indiana; and Stockton, California. This change was brought about because of the heavy demand for Dodge cars. The plant simply did not have enough capacity to produce both.

This move also marked the end of production of Dodge commercials built by the original Dodge Brothers Company. From this point until the purchase of Dodge by Chrysler, all truck production was badged as Graham Brothers, even though by this time Graham Brothers was a wholly owned division of Dodge Brothers.

On June 26, 1926, production began on a redesigned three-quarter-ton panel and screenside. An oblong window was added just back of the driver's seat—a Graham Brothers trademark. The rear-axle ratio was lowered to provide higher speeds and faster acceleration.

5. April 14, 1927: Trucks in the commercial line of Graham Brothers were given the newly redesigned and improved engine called the No. 124. Changes included chain drive in place of timing

gears, oil pump inside the crankcase, and both manifolds on the engine's right side. In addition, the water pump, generator, and distributor were moved. Bore and stroke remained the same, but with a compression ratio of 5.3:1, the engine's output was now pegged at 60-brake horsepower (bhp).

First Dodge Pickup

In 1924 Dodge Brothers brought out its first factory-built pickup and its first factory-built stake as companions to the screenside and panel. Both new commercial models featured 6ft bodies constructed of wood. An open and a closed cab were offered for both new trucks.

Sales totals for the 8ft panel, stake, and pickup never exceeded more than 200-300 per model per year. The pickup and stake were built only from 1924-1926, and the 8ft panel only in 1925 and 1926.

'Fast Four' Panel

After an absence of several years, a half-ton truck returned in 1927. This was the Graham Brothers SD half-ton Fast Four panel. Its 108in-wheelbase chassis and engine were the same as the Fast Four passenger cars. Its Dodge Brothers 124 engine gave the SD the same lively performance as the Dodge Brothers famous car, "The Fastest Four in America."

The Fast Four half-ton panel's cargo area was only 66in long by 45in wide by 40in high. Its rear cargo door was a single door like that on a sedan

Nothing is known about this pert 1931 Dodge roadster pickup except that a quantity of this model were built, probably for a fleet buyer.

16

delivery, and it had two rear glass windows. This was a snappy looking little rig with excellent performance to boot.

Commercial Conversions

In mid-February 1927, Dodge Brothers announced a commercial conversion for sedans, coupes, and roadsters. Commercial conversions don't interest collectors because they are indeed passenger vehicles, but should be at least mentioned here because they do double as commercials. Conversions were popular for a number of years lasting late into the thirties. They served as a dual purpose vehicle for the business owner who, for whatever reasons, desired to use his automobile for both personal and business use. Most conversions consisted of a slide-out-type pickup box for coupes and roadsters, and often also consisted of some type of drawer or compartment arrangements for organizing parts, parcels, and literature; a very handy device indeed for the traveling salesman. Conversions could be made by the dealer or ordered directly from the factory. Dodge's sedan conversion, also called an All-Purpose sedan, was available only from the factory and was converted by the Millspaugh and Irish Company. Its rear seat was removable and it had a sedan delivery-type rear door for ease of loading.

In 1927 and 1928 (the last years for the Graham Brothers trucks), they produced trucks of half, three-quarter-, one-, one-and-a-half-, and two-ton capacities. In 1928 a three-ton model was added. The one-ton was the famous Graham Brothers' "G-Boy" truck.

Dodge Brothers Four-Cylinder Engine

Dodge Brothers' dependable four-cylinder engine was the only engine to power Dodge and Graham Brothers trucks from 1914-1928. The Dodge Brothers' new six-cylinder automobile engine was released for two-ton Graham Brothers trucks for 1928. The original four-cylinder Dodge engine remained the same without noteable change from 1914 until September 2, 1926 (the 1927 model year), when the updated four with five main bearings was adopted for all Dodge Brothers and Graham Brothers trucks. The change to five mains did not affect the engine's output or displacement. In 1927 the new model 124 engine replaced the original four main bearing engine in cars, trucks, and commercials (on March 22, 1927, for cars; and on April 14, 1927, for commercials and trucks. The 124 engine retained the original bore and stroke and the five mains. But now a chain drive replaced the original timing gears; the oil pump was moved inside the crankcase; both manifolds were mounted on the engine's right side; and the water pump, generator, and distributor were mounted in new places. A boost in compression ratio raised the engine's power output. This engine and the cars they

This 1932 Dodge half-ton panel is typical of Dodge-built panels up to 1933.

powered were called the Fast Fours due to the great boost in performance over the original four. All four-cylinder auto production ceased on July 23, 1928, which was only four days before Walter Chrysler purchased Dodge Brothers. The Dodge Brothers company built a total of 2,019,544 four-cylinder vehicles, and it is estimated that 365,441 of the total were Dodge Brothers and Graham Brothers commercials.

Four-Cylinder Engine Specifications

Dodge four-cylinder engine specifications are as follows:

For 1914-September 1926, the bore and stroke was 3 7/8 x 4 1/2, resulting in a displacement of 212.3ci, 35 brake horsepower (bhp), and a compression ratio of 4.0:1. The engine used four main bearings and solid valve lifters.

The specs were the same for September 1926-April 1927, except with five main bearings.

For April 1927 to the end of production, the bore and stroke were 3 7/8 x 4 1/2, the displacement was 212.3ci, it produced 44bhp, had a compression ratio of 4.1:1, five main bearings and solid valve lifters.

Chrysler

Walter Chrysler closed the deal of his life when in July 1928 the final papers were signed, giving Chrysler ownership of the much larger Dodge Brothers Company. Dodge Brothers then became a division of the Chrysler Corporation. Chrysler Corp. acquired all the assets of Dodge Brothers, including all Graham Brothers truck factories.

At the time of the Dodge Brothers buyout, the 1929 Graham models were set. Early in January 1929, all Graham Brothers trucks were renamed Dodge Brothers.

By mid-year in 1929, the first partially "Chryslerized" trucks were introduced. The first was a re-worked half-ton panel. It now sported a 109in-wheelbase chassis with the 175.4ci Plymouth four-cylinder engine. Styling was practically unchanged from the SD and it was priced at $795.

The stylish new Merchants Express stood out with its fine appearance. The panel was painted blue with black fenders, gray interior, and wheels painted cream with black hubs. The radiator and headlight rims were chrome. It was a favorite with salesmen, for it gave them the ride and performance of a car.

Shortly thereafter a new series of four-cylinder one-ton models was announced—with the four-cylinder being the same Plymouth engine as in the half-ton. A six was also available for one-tonners.

From 1929 through 1932, the Dodge light-duty lineup stayed generally intact with only minor engineering and appearance updates. These were the early years of the Depression, and the challenge was one of survival. Survival meant building the best-quality trucks possible for the money and keeping expenses under strict control.

This 1932 pickup is the last of the Pioneer Era trucks. Very few of these trucks have survived.

Chapter 2

Glamour Era Trucks 1933-1935

★★★★★	1933-1935 Commercial pickup
★★★	1933-1935 Commercial panel
★★★★	1933-1935 Commercial Westchester Suburban
★★★	1933-1935 Commercial sedan and dual-purpose sedan
★★★★	1933-1935 Commercial canopy and screenside
★★	1933-1935 Three-quarter- and one-ton pickup, panel, and screenside

Chances are we would all agree that superior styling, or beauty, has a direct bearing on how well a new car will do in the automobile sales war. The question for truck owners is whether the same is true for trucks. Will a better-looking truck drive sales up? Superior styling of its commercial cars and trucks was Dodge management's marketing strategy for the 1933 model year. Dodge sales had suffered greatly in 1932; in fact, sales were at the same level they had been the first full year of truck production—back in 1919!

If we look at the historical record, we find that sales for the truck industry increased by 146 percent in 1933 over 1932's dismal totals (figures are

The Glamour Era trucks were the first trucks fully engineered and styled by Chrysler Corporation's engineers and designers. Front sheet metal styling was shared with Dodge autos. This pickup is a 1933 model.

The wooden-bodied Westchester Suburban was built on the long-wheelbase commercial chassis.

This attractive 1933 looked right at home on America's finest bouvelards.

for a calendar year). Dodge truck sales in 1933 posted a whopping increase of 362 percent over 1932. We can logically conclude, then, that Dodge's exceedingly glamorous new style accounted for the bulk of this increase.

There are a couple of issues here, however, that raw numbers don't reveal. For instance, at the start of the 1933 model year, Dodge carried over all 1932 models until the new models were ready. It was not until January that the first new model was

Commercial sedans were two-door Dodge sedans converted to commercial use by blanking out the

rear side windows and adding a sedan-delivery-type rear door. These trucks are extremely rare.

released, the commercial sedan. The commercial panel and commercial pickup followed in February. The medium-duty ton-and-a-half models came out in May and two-tonners in June. One has to wonder how sales would have been if all models had been available at the normal new model introduction time of early fall.

The issue that actually worked to the benefit of Dodge is that in 1933 the best-selling light-duty truck was the panel, not the pickup as it is today. Dodge just happened to have the best game in town in its new double-level or "humpback" panel. Dodge promoted the unique new panel heavily in advertising and promotions, and their efforts paid off in a big way. If you study American light-truck history, you will find that the best-selling trucks from the very beginning up into the forties were the screensides and panels. These trucks were preferred by package delivery firms, traveling salesmen, tradesmen, bakeries, florists, and many other types of businesses. Try finding a

John Cadwallader, the owner of this 1934 commercial pickup, uses it to promote his glass business. Its yellow wire wheels and wide, white sidewalls cause this truck to stand out in a crowd. *Tom Brownell*

In the Glamour Era, the commercial screenside was a covered pickup without a barrier between the driver and the load space. Note that the roofline is about level with the top of the windshield, as opposed to the roof of the double-level commercial panel.

William and Norma Haske of Wisconsin Rapids, Wisconsin, said, "We took it all apart, stripped it to the bones, took off every speck of paint and primer. A friend of ours painted it, and we put it back together." What a beautiful second series 1935 KC Pickup!

Dodge pickup ad from the thirties. They are almost nonexistent; mostly what you'll find are ads for commercial panels and commercial sedans.

The Glamour Era light-duty trucks were the last of Dodge's Commercial cars. That is, the new commercial models were built on an automobile's frame, shared front-end sheet metal styling with Dodge cars, and used many automobile mechanical components. The commercial cars differed from passenger cars in one important way: They did not change for change's sake from one model year to the next. So while a 1933 Dodge car and commercial car looked identical from the front, by the end of the Glamour Era, in 1935, the resemblance was no longer a mirror image. Appearance and mechanical improvements on commercial cars between 1933 and 1935 were minimal. The only two changes of real importance are: the addition of full-length water jackets to the all-new L-6 engine in 1934; and, in mid-year 1935, significant changes to the cab included moving the door hinges from the rear to the front, and the cab's roof was upgraded to all steel.

All New 1933s

The 1933 commercial cars from Dodge were unique because they comprised a new truck line that was new from the wheels up, a real rarity. The Glamour Era's frames, engine, bodies, and interiors were all new. Also of some importance to the collector is that these trucks were designed and engineered by Chrysler Corp. And this was the first year the customer could not purchase a four-cylinder engine in a new Dodge truck.

Research on Dodge light-duty trucks owned by collectors reveals that the Glamour Era accounts

The three-quarter-ton and one-ton series light-duty trucks were made by building down ton-and-a-half trucks with lighter springs and smaller wheels and tires. Their appearance was the same as the medium-duty models. Note the unusual side door on this double-level panel.

The second series 1935 commercial pickup's cab had an all-steel roof and front-hinged doors. Dodge used this cab through the 1938 model year. No other styling changes of note were introduced on the second series trucks. The collector should be aware that only the commercial pickup was given the new cab.

A ton-and-a-half canopy. Note its larger wheels. This truck could be a 1933, 1934, or early 1935.

During the 1935 model year, hood-side nameplates were changed from "Dodge Brothers" to "Dodge."

for only 2.6 percent of total collector trucks. While that is a paltry figure, the percentage for the Pioneer Era is only 1.6 percent!

Collectability

All Glamour Era models are highly recommended to the collector. These trucks are extremely rare and are also of interest due to their rich good looks. Mechanical parts are surprisingly readily available. Body parts and trim are another matter, but if the collector is diligent these parts can be found, either used or as new old stock .

The discriminating collector who wants the rarest of the rare should search for a long-wheelbase second series 1935 pickup. Two wheelbases were used during this era. The short wheelbase of 111 1/4in was the same as the car's chassis and was standard for all but the commercial panel, which rode on a 119in wheelbase. In mid-year 1935, when the change was made to the new cab, management made the decision to build the com-

mercial pickup on both wheelbases. The long-wheelbase pickup, which was still a commercial car, or half-ton, featured a correspondingly longer pickup box. I know of only one of these pickups, but no doubt more are out there for the collector who wants to make the effort to locate one.

1934

Three new offerings were made this year. A clever new "dual-purpose" commercial sedan was intended for salesmen and delivery men. It was essentially the commercial sedan from 1933, but this model had a removable upholstered rear seat that could be inserted through the large rear sedan-delivery-type door to convert the commercial car to a passenger car.

The other two new offerings were a commercial screenside and commercial canopy.

Two mechanical upgrades of note were the drop-forged I-beam front axle in place of the origi-

We know this three-quarter- and one-ton milk delivery is a 1935 by its new "Dodge" nameplate.

This custom, long-wheelbase hearse was built on an extended chassis. The rounded ends of its front bumper tell us that this is a 1935 truck.

nal round tubular type, and the engine bored out to displace 201.3ci. The rear axle ratio was increased to 4.11:1, which gave much quicker acceleration and faster road speeds.

1935

There were no changes other than those already noted. The pickup box on the long-wheelbase model is 70 3/4in versus 62 3/4in for the short wheelbase pickup.

Prices were: $480 for the pickup; canopy, $590; screen, $610; sedan, $595; dual-purpose sedan, $780; Westchester Suburban, $745; and panel $595.

Dodge Ram Hood Ornament

The Glamour Era was the first Dodge truck series to display the now-famous Dodge Ram hood ornament. The Ram hood ornament and spare tire

lock were always shipped with each truck unless the dealer's order specified otherwise. The list price on the Ram hood ornament in 1935 was an outrageous $2.00!

Glamour Era Truck Engines					
Year	Bore x Stroke	CID	BHP	Torque	Compression
For Commercial series trucks					
1933	3 1/8 x 4 1/8	189.8	70 @ 3600	130lb/ft	5.5
1934-1935	3 1/8 x 4 3/8	201.3	70 @ 3000	138lb/ft	5.8
For three-quarter and one-ton models					
1934-1935	3 1/4 x 4 3/8	217.7	70 @ 3000	150lb/ft	5.6

Note: Early in the calendar year when the new three-quarter and one-ton series was first announced, it shared the 201.3ci engine with the commercial line; in the spring its engine was changed to the larger and more powerful 217.7.

Chapter 3

Truck-Built Era Trucks 1936-1938

★★★★★	1936-1938 Commercial pickup
★★★★	1936-1938 Commercial panel
★★★★	1936-1938 Westchester Suburban
★★★	1936-1938 Sedan and dual-purpose sedan
★★★★	1936-1938 Canopy and screenside
★★★	1937-1938 Three-quarter- and one-ton pickup, platform, stake, panel, canopy

The Truck-Built Era was another watershed era for Dodge because this was the first time Dodge light-duty trucks were mounted on big, straight, and husky truck-type double-drop frame rails with five heavy cross members. Even so, official terminology continued to refer to light-duty trucks as commercial cars. In the conservative truck business, old ways die hard.

The obvious reason for switching to a truck-type frame was to make these hard-working Dodge trucks even sturdier and better able to handle big loads. A second reason was that a truck-type frame was better suited for mounting special bodies onto a chassis cab, making this an improvement that greatly expanded Dodge's truck market.

The only exception to the above was the commercial sedan. The sedan was really more passenger car than truck. It continued to be built on a car's chassis; in fact, it was a car slightly modified to make it suitable to carry a light load. It also was powered by a Dodge passenger car's "Red Ram" 218 L-6 engine, while the commercial cars were powered by the same 201 L-6 as in previous years.

Sales figures are not available by model; if they were, we would probably find that sales of the sedan were not real brisk. Dodge's commercial

The Truck-Built Era's cab was carried over from the second series 1935 models, but all other sheet metal was new. The pickup shown here is a 1936 half-ton.

The double-level panel carried over from the Glamour Era. This high-line 1936 panel is equipped with an extra-cost chrome radiator shell and chrome headlights.

The three-quarter-ton and one-ton double-level panel also carried over for 1936. This truck has an interesting body addition designed to promote its owner's business.

This three-quarter-ton and one-ton canopy has a custom aftermarket canopy body. For 1936 Dodge built three-quarter-ton and one-ton panels, pickups, and screensides. As in the Glamour Era, these were ton-and-a-half trucks built with lighter components.

sedan sold for $665 versus $590 for Ford's sedan delivery and $535 for Chevrolet's sedan delivery. This price spread in 1936 was significant. Also, many business owners didn't want their delivery man driving a more expensive delivery car than the car they drove.

This 1936 half-ton pickup was photographed at the 1988 Sloan's Festival in Flint, Michigan. *Ron Cenowa.*

In spite of the fact that Dodge commercials were now built like a truck, they still featured automobile-type styling. The front end of a 1936 Dodge truck looked very much the same as the new Dodge cars. Good styling sold trucks in the Glamour Era, so management stayed with a proven concept. In fact, Dodge truck literature and advertising stressed a "Beauty Styling" theme.

As noted earlier, the cab was new beginning late in the 1935 model year; it was also, of course, the cab for the Truck-Built Era. Dodge pioneered the all-steel cab (a cab welded into one solid unit for greater safety, longer life, and a quieter ride). Dodge touted its steel cab as the "Safety-Steel Cab." The all-steel cab is a real plus for the restorer, because he doesn't have the extra work of replacing a number of pieces of wood when restoring his truck's cab.

Fore-Point Load Distribution

One important new feature of the Truck-Built commercials—and an advancement that makes them a truly modern truck—was what Dodge termed "fore-point" load distribution. Fore-point load distribution was a big step ahead in truck engineering, as it moved the center of the load forward to distribute the truck's weight more equally

In 1937 the Chalker Laundry in Rensselaer, New York, owned these three double-level half-ton pan- els. From left to right, they are a 1933, a 1937, and a 1936.

on front and rear axles. This was accomplished by moving the engine, cab, and body forward in rela- tion to the axles. Since the cab was moved forward, cab-to-rear-axle distances were increased consider- ably. The center of the body was now ahead of the rear axle. Moving greater weight to the front in- creased the weight on the front tires, which im- proved steering and front wheel braking. Fore- point weight distribution also allowed for in- creased wheelbase lengths. For commercial cars, for example, the pickup's wheelbase increased from 111in to 116in. Fore-point weight distribution is clearly seen in the more pleasing, modern ap- pearance of the Truck-Built truck's front styling.

New Three-Quarter and One-Ton Models

Some confusion surrounds the three-quarter and one-ton Dodge trucks of the Truck-Built era. For the first year of this era, Dodge followed the pattern established in the Glamour Era: The three- quarter and one-ton models were actually ton-and- a-half trucks, but equipped with lighter springs, wheels, and tires. At this time in Dodge truck his- tory, a ton-and-a-half pickup, panel, and canopy

were standard offerings. These three ton-and-a- half models (built with lighter springs, wheels, and tires) comprised the three-quarter and one-ton of- ferings. We have to keep in mind that standard load ratings in the thirties were a lot lower than now. Today's three-quarter and one-ton trucks are capable of handling loads larger than the ton-and- a-half models carried back in the thirties.

In 1936 Dodge offered two levels of ton-and-a- half trucks—a heavy series and a light series. The heavy series was powered by a 218 engine, had standard dual rears, and was rated at 11,500lb gross vehicle weight (GVW). The lighter series looked the same in terms of styling, but was pow- ered by a 201 engine, was available only with sin- gle rears, and had a GVW that topped 7,000lb. The three-quarter and one-ton series came from this lighter series. The three-quarter-ton series was grossed at 5,700lb and the one-ton series at 6,200lb. Only three models were offered (the panel, canopy/screen, and pickup) and only on 136in

This exquisite 1937 half-ton pickup in original con- dition was owned until just recently by Greg Lindahl of Minneapolis, Minnesota.

The only visual difference between 1936 and 1937 was in the grille. In 1936 grille bars were vertical; and in 1937, as seen in this 1937 pickup, the grille bars were horizontal.

29

In mid-year 1937, the styling of three-quarter-ton and one-ton trucks was changed to the same as that of half-ton models. Shown here is a 1937 three-quarter- and one-ton with a special hearse body.

wheelbases. The three-quarter-ton models were built for a 5,700lb GVW and the one-ton models for 6,200lb GVW. In other words, these three-quarter and one-ton trucks looked like the ton-and-a-half trucks of their day, but could only haul lighter loads. Dodge advertised them for the business that had bulky but light loads to carry. All models were fitted with 9ft bodies, pickup included.

1937

Dodge Truck Division's management began the 1937 model year by announcing several impor-

Truck-Built Era Engines					
For Commercials and three-quarter-ton and one-ton trucks					
Year	Bore x Stroke	CID	BHP	Torque	Compression
1936	3 1/8 x 4 3/8	201.3	70 @ 3000	138lb/ft	5.8
1937-1938	3 3/8 x 4 1/16	218.06	75 @ 3000	155lb/ft	6.5

The only styling change for 1938 was a new grille, as seen on this 1938 half-ton pickup.

tant and significant improvements, a move that would not be repeated until the 1973 model year, thirty-six years later.

Normally in the year following the introduction of an all-new model lineup, there will be only very minor, if any, changes, additions, or improvements to the line.

But this was not to be a normal year. Instead, Dodge management placed the three-quarter and one-ton model lineup in the logical order with which we are familiar. Here is what happened: The ton-and-a-half series was shortened to a chassis cab, stake, and a 133in-wheelbase, 9ft pickup only. Gone were the panel, canopy, and screen. These models were moved down to become the three-quarter and one-ton series.

The three-quarter and one-ton MD Series was now structured as follows: A panel, canopy, and screen were available on a 136in wheelbase chassis. A stake, platform, and pickup could be ordered on either a 120in or 136in wheelbase chassis. Because all chassis, engines, transmissions, and axle specifications were the same for all models, Dodge management classified every model as a three-quarter and one-ton. The maximum GVW for all models was 6,000lb. The short-wheelbase chassis carried a 7ft body and the long chassis, a 9ft body.

Safety Cabs

It may strike you that 1937 was very early for Dodge engineers to be concerned with keeping the driver safe in the event of a crash. In 1937, Dodge engineers learned from plastic surgeons that many injuries resulted from projections on dashboards and elsewhere in vehicle interiors, and the engineers designed a new instrument panel with all controls set flush—a new safety advantage for dri-

This huge 1938 three-quarter-ton and one-ton pickup carried a 9ft cargo box on a 136in wheelbase.

vers. The entire dash was free from projections; even the windshield crank was set flush into the panel.

Dodge's new "High-Safety Steel" cab was driver-designed in other ways, too. For example, the cab's interior was beautifully trimmed throughout and fully lined to give it a finished look—no bare, painted steel. And, of course, its cab was made entirely of steel, braced and cross-braced and welded into one solid unit.

Express Trucks Renamed Pickups

A piece of Dodge truck trivia the collector will find interesting is that this was the first year Dodge literature used the term *pickup*. Sometimes the word was hyphenated (*pick-up*), and other times not. And to make the issue more confusing, sometimes the term *express* was used instead. Actually, the terms *pickup* and *express* continued well into the fifties, when the word *pickup* gradually replaced *express*.

Dodge's famous double-level panel ceased to exist after 1938. These unique trucks are a favorite with collectors.

Chapter 4

Job-Rated Era Trucks 1939-1947

★★★★★	1939-1947 Half-ton pickup
★★★	1939-1947 Half-ton panel
★★★★★	1939-1947 Half-ton canopy
★★★	1939-1947 Three-quarter- and one-ton pickup
★★★	1939-1947 Three-quarter- and one-ton stake and platform
★★★	1939-1947 One-ton panel
★★★★	1939-1947 One-ton canopy

This era built the trucks most favored by collectors. It accounts for fully one-third of the light-duty Dodge trucks in their hands. The most popular truck built by Dodge in the Job-Rated Era—or any era—is the WC half-ton pickup. The majority of these trucks are post-war models, which is logical because more trucks were built in the post-war years, and pre-war trucks were most often worked to death. The second most popular Dodges of this period are the World War II military trucks, which are covered in chapter ten. Let's look at the civilian Dodge trucks of this era in depth to see what makes them so special.

We saw in the Glamour Era that Dodge placed a lot of emphasis on building a very smart-appearing truck. When a new truck was introduced in 1936, the same emphasis on appearance was continued. The official position of Dodge Truck management in 1936 was that, "Other things being equal, the truck which is smartly styled and mod-

A half-ton 1939 chassis cab is ready for a body builder to mount a special body.

The panel for 1939 was changed considerably. The exclusive Dodge double-level type was now histo-ry. This florist's 1939 half-ton panel had interesting grille guards mounted on its front bumper.

ern in appearance is of far greater value to the operation. It attracts favorable attention 'on the job,' it is a traveling advertisement, it classifies the owner as being successful. It helps get business."

The 1936 and 1937 models are two of the better-looking trucks Dodge ever built, but something happened in 1938. Many believe the good looks associated with Dodge trucks disappeared. The new grille in 1938 just didn't have it. Which may explain why very few 1938 trucks were sold. In all fairness, I have to point out that the roof fell in on the economy in 1938 and total truck sales dropped like a rock. Total truck sales fell by 44 percent, and Dodge sales dipped by 56 percent. That figure makes a statement about how well Dodge's 1938 styling was received—or more accurately, not received!

New Styling

First and foremost, the Job-Rated Era enabled Dodge to get back on the right styling track. This new truck was smart looking. Its beauty and graceful proportions and smooth streamlining created an eye-compelling, up-to-the-minute attractiveness that commanded attention. Remember that the thirties was the era of streamlining (that is, a vehicle had to appear to be moving even when

stopped). It was a requirement for all new boats, cars, trains, and especially airplanes to be streamlined. Chrysler's own Airflow autos of earlier in the decade are an excellent example of streamlining.

An important design element that helped create the streamlined appearance can be seen in the

This bread delivery built on a 1939 half-ton chassis looks somewhat odd due to its short body. The body abruptly terminated immediately behind the rear wheel openings.

This 1939 half-ton pickup was designated a TC. In 1940 the half-ton pickup was a VC, and from 1941 through 1947 it became a WC.

long, gently rounded headlights. Also note the four speed-lines, or ridges, on the lower rear sections of the front and rear fenders of the WC pickup. The openings in the grille that flow back on either side of a central, vertical, chrome strip suggested speed and movement, as did the hood louvers, which extended horizontally along the side of the long, sweeping hood. And lastly, Dodge's first-ever V-shaped windshield gave the impression that these trucks were more than able to cut through the air.

New Cab

Appearance was not Dodge engineers' only consideration when they designed the Job-Rated Era trucks. Comfort was high on their priority list, too. To create more driver comfort, the seat was redesigned and covered in a leather-looking vinyl (which was blue, by the way). And to make a more comfortable driving position, the seat was now adjustable to three positions—the idea was to make it fit the requirements of short, average, and tall drivers. The entire cab interior was lined to protect the driver from severe heat and cold and to give the cab an easier-to-live-with feeling. Dodge cabs in previous years had been lined (with soft cardboard for better appearance and more comfort), but in 1939 a dash liner was also added. Another new feature that was most welcomed by drivers was the increased size of the new cab; it was almost 4in wider, and taller, too. There was plenty of room for a two-man crew on the new wider seat cushion.

Driver Safety

Drivers were concerned with safety, too, and here again the new Dodge cab did not disappoint. The cab in which the driver sat was safe because it was of strong, welded steel construction. No wood was used anywhere in this cab. The safe-interior trend begun in 1937 continued with 1939's "High Safety" interior. This meant all control knobs, as well as the ignition key, were recessed. The "High" had to do with the fact that the dashboard was set high enough to be well above knee height to prevent them from bumping into the dash in the event of a sudden stop. All instruments were grouped at the left, directly in the driver's line of vision, allowing him to glance over the instruments without taking his eyes from the road for more than an instant. The convenient glove compartment at the

This 1939 half-ton pickup is owned by Ron Ashley of Prineville, Oregon. It is a very rare truck because few 1939s have survived. Ron completely restored it in 1981, and, in fact, he found many of its parts in the county dump!

It's easy to understand the utility afforded by this 1940 one-ton canopy. The helper could readily access the load along the length of its body through the open canvas cover. In the Job-Rated Era, Dodge also built one-ton pickups, stakes, platforms, and panels.

right was opened by means of a recessed hand-hold in the door, rather than the conventional protruding knob. Both doors locked from the interior, but only the right could be key-locked from outside. A decided safety advantage, its purpose was to keep the driver away from moving traffic.

Design Shortcoming

Dodge designers made a valiant effort in styling the new Job-Rated Era trucks, but unfortunately they missed the mark just a little. The problem was that the chrome trim detail on the front of the grille was not quite right. If you have noticed, the styling of Dodge's passenger cars and trucks in 1939 was very similar—the overall styling theme was the same for both vehicles. It is interesting that the design elements that were common to both looked quite good on the car, whereas on the truck they fell flat. One design element, the low-mounted chrome detail on the very front of the grille, though a disappointment on medium- and heavy-duty trucks, was in reality not bad on half-ton trucks. This weakness was corrected in 1940 by a minor change in the chrome trim. The problem in 1939 was that the chrome bars were located too low on the front of the grille. This tended to make the trucks look smaller, because the chrome's location drew the eye down. The original idea was to draw the eye up and back in a sweeping motion to give the impression of streamlining and speed. The new design corrected the problem. By simply moving the whole chrome detail higher up on the grille and changing the horizontal bars to straight lines, the front end now took on a more massive, rugged look while maintaining the streamlined look.

Styling for 1940

Two other styling notes for 1940 completed the new look. First, the chrome-plated Dodge nameplates were removed from the top front peaks of the grille and replaced by the name *Dodge* in raised chrome letters in the center of the new grille. The surrounding areas were painted red. Second, because the headlights were changed to the improved, new, sealed beam units, a small parking light was mounted on top of each headlight bucket.

1941 Styling

Three minor styling changes were made for the 1941 model year. The Job-Rated Era's styling was then set and remained for the balance of the era. The first change was to rework the grille one last time to eliminate the horizontal grille bars just below the Dodge nameplate. For 1941 and in early

A dependable Dodge 1941 one-ton pickup was selected by the fire department in Buena Park, California.

Only in 1941, and for a short time in 1942, were chrome strips applied along the lower horizontal grille openings. The Haller Baking Company made a wise and timely purchase when they contracted for 100 half-ton panels in November 1941.

1942 only, four horizontal chrome bars were added to the lower grille aprons. The second change was moving the parking lights from the top of the headlights to the cowls. Third and lastly, the headlight buckets were moved out to the crown of the front fenders for better illuminating.

New Truck Plant

Dodge Truck management came out of the blocks charging hard into the Job-Rated Era, for they had just christened an all-new plant in Warren, Michigan. It was the most modern, exclusive

This Detroit area Dodge and Plymouth dealer employed a 1941 half-ton pickup for service work. Note the spiffy, double front bumpers—evidently intended to protect the grille when used to push vehicles.

truck plant then in existence, and this huge factory had the largest production capacity of any plant in the country dedicated to truck building. The new plant began production of 1939 models in October 1938.

Job-Rated Chassis

The Job-Rated Era trucks, although all new in styling, retained most of the former chassis and mechanical components from 1938. However, the frames of 1939 Dodge trucks were stronger because they used a steel with increased tensile strength. In addition, the side rails were extended forward, giving more solid support to the bumper and increasing front-end rigidity. The bumpers themselves were also stronger, as they were the channel type made from heavy steel stock. This new front bumper became in effect an additional cross member, adding strength to the entire front. Engines and transmissions carried over without change.

Job-Rated

Since this is the Job-Rated Era, I should give an explanation of what Dodge meant by *job-rated*. The concept was quite simple. *Job-rated* meant fitting the truck to the job. In other words, it was a matter of selling the customer the truck chassis model that most closely fit his needs. If his new truck was too small, it wouldn't perform well. If it was too big, he paid for more truck than was necessary. *Job-rated* did not mean that a customer could choose from a menu of engines, transmissions, etc. Rather, it meant he could pick out the Dodge truck model that most closely matched his needs from a total of 112 standard chassis and body models on eighteen wheelbase lengths from a light-duty half-ton to a heavy-duty three-ton.

A consumer could customize his new truck, but only to a degree. For example, if he wanted to purchase a pickup, he could choose either a half-, three-quarter-, or a one-ton model. Pickup engines were standard, with one engine for the half-ton and a larger standard engine for the three-quarter and one-tons. But he could choose the standard three-speed transmission or the optional four-speed transmission. In addition, he could choose heavier front and rear springs and larger tires, or an optional rear axle ratio. That was the limit of his options. You are probably saying, "That's no big deal." You're right. Job-rated was Dodge management's way of promoting the hundreds of available models.

New Model Lineup

The logical half-, three-quarter-, and one-ton model lineup of light-duty trucks that we are now so accustomed to was put into place with 1939's T-Series. The half-ton trucks were TC models. *T* meaning the 1939 model year and *C* for half-ton, but notice the *C* is a carryover from the old commercial car days. Models available in half-ton capacities included a pickup, panel, canopy, and screen. All rode on a 116in wheelbase and were powered by the 201 engine.

Under the three-quarter-ton category we have the TD-15 models. The *D* designated both three-quarter-ton and one-ton models. It wasn't until 1948 and the B-Series that the three-quarter-tonners became C models and only the one-tonners were Ds. Three-quarter-ton models consisted of a pickup, stake, and platform. They rode on a 120in wheelbase, and their engine was the 218 L-6.

In the one-ton lineup we have two series: the TD-20 series on a 120in wheelbase consisting of a pickup, stake, and platform, and the TD-21 series with a 133in wheelbase; it included a panel, screenside, canopy, stake, platform, and pickup. All one-ton models were powered by the same engine as the three-quarter-ton trucks.

New Half-Ton Pickup Cargo Box

Dodge engineers completely reworked the half-ton pickup's box for 1939. For starters, the box was made both wider and longer. Previously its width was just under 48in; now it measured 48.25in—big enough to carry a piece of 4ft-wide building board flat on its floor with the tailgate down. Its length was stretched from 6ft to 6.5ft. Height of the sides remained at 17in with steel stake pockets.

The other major change in the pickup's box was the use of 13/16in oak planks with steel skid strips on the floor. The engineers believed wood was superior to steel because a wood plank could be easily replaced in the event it became damaged. The handsome appearance and practical utility of these pickups are attested to by their great appeal to today's collectors.

1940

Here is another question for you Dodge trivia buffs. What was the first year Dodge half-ton models were equipped with wheel bolts made in right-hand and left-hand threads? 1940. Several years ago I read a statement by a writer who preferred another make of pickup. He chided Dodge for using this idea, which he thought was rather silly. What he didn't know was that back in this period Dodge was not alone; other truck manufacturers also equipped their trucks with this same safety device. The most notable name among the heavy-duty truck manufacturers who also equipped their trucks with right- and left-hand threads was Mack! Dodge Truck's superior engineering wins again!

Rare Panels

The collector who wants to find the most interesting and desirable 1940 panel model should search for what Dodge called the "Fifth Avenue" panel. It was equipped with a special group of options to create a panel with "Ultra Smartness." This panel was aimed at those specialty and/or upscale retailers who wanted delivery equipment with the very finest appearance. All truck manufacturers at this time promoted the idea that a smart-looking delivery truck was good for a businessman's business. A Fifth Avenue panel was equipped with a "messenger's seat" (rather than an ordinary auxiliary seat), chrome-plated windshield frames and headlights, chrome wheel covers even for one-ton models, formal side lamps, and special "flexible-action" (soft) springs.

This 1941 half-ton panel is only one of several low-mileage, original condition Dodge trucks in Ron Cenowa's collection.

This photo taken on October 10, 1945, shows "black-out" model civilian trucks being built. These trucks are extremely rare and are eagerly sought by collectors.

Don and Becky Evans of Bakersfield, California, restored this elegant red and black 1947 Dodge WD 20 one-ton pickup.

1941

In 1940 we saw Dodge Truck management promoting the Fifth Avenue panel for retailers who demanded a smart-looking truck for door-to-door package delivery work. Now in 1941 we will see how Dodge Truck management again moved in the direction of increasing the advertising value of all light-duty truck models.

As a no-cost option for any half-, three-quarter-, or one-ton truck, a buyer could now choose to have his new Dodge painted in any number of attractive two-tone color combinations. The standard paint scheme for all Dodge trucks prior to 1941

This rare 1947 half-ton canopy was restored by Dave and Judy Truax of Prescott, Wisconsin. This red and black beauty is a consistent first-place trophy winner.

was to paint the body, cab, and hood one of several standard colors and the lower grille, fenders, and running boards black. The front bumper was always painted argent (aluminum). Or, as an extra-cost option, a buyer could order his truck painted one color. The two-tone no-cost scheme allowed the buyer to order his truck painted in any of two colors. The body, cab, and hood would be painted one color and the lower grille and fenders the second color. Running boards were always black and the bumper argent. A second no-cost option was to paint the entire truck one color. The standard colors were Dodge Truck Dark Blue, Gray, Green, Light Blue, Orange, and Red.

De Luxe Cab Option

These were exciting times at Dodge Truck, for management was not only concerned with building the most attractive, quality-engineered trucks, but also in beginning the long, slow road to making trucks more amenable to the driver's comfort and safety. The De Luxe Cab option was the first meaningful effort to upgrade the cab's interior for driver comfort, productivity, and safety.

Mechanical Considerations

Only one item of note here. For better performance and longer engine life, an oil-bath air filter became standard. No change in the engine lineup for light-duty models.

1942

No appearance changes, even the two-tone no-charge paint option, were carried over for 1942. The few mechanical improvements included a new engine (a 218 L-6) for half- and three-quarter-ton models. A new 230 L-6 was made available for the one-ton series. The only other improvement was a change to a thicker stock for the fabrication of half-tons' frames.

All civilian truck production ceased in April 1942. Very few 1942 Dodge truck models have survived, probably because the total produced in the 1942 calendar year was only 18,658. These trucks were subjected to a lot of use and abuse during the war years and after, until civilian truck production was brought up to speed.

1945-1947

Civilian truck production ceased in 1942 when all Chrysler plants, along with those of all other auto and truck manufacturers, turned their attention to the war effort. Dodge military trucks are covered in chapter ten. No Dodge civilian trucks were built in 1943. In 1944 the government allowed Dodge Truck to begin limited production of ton-and-a-half trucks; most of these were cab-over-en-

A left rear-quarter view of a 1947 half-ton pickup shows its underslung spare tire carrier. Note also that the embossed Dodge name on the tailgate is painted argent.

gine (COE) models. It is somewhat of an oddity in that only Dodge of the big three was allowed to build COEs at this time.

In 1945 the government again allowed Dodge to build ton-and-a-half trucks for civilian use. A purchaser had to prove that he needed the truck to perform work critical to the war effort. By the way, these civilian trucks were built alongside military trucks, on the same line. The first civilian pickup, a half-ton model, was built on April 11, 1945. This pickup was what was called a "blackout" model. That is, all parts that were chrome plated in normal times were painted in order to save chrome for defense-related production. Almost immediately after the war in the Pacific ended, Dodge was allowed to change over to building civilian trucks. Dodge was able to convert its Detroit truck plant to volume output of civilian production in a record-breaking two hours!

1946-1947 Models

Dodge's 1946 model lineup was the same as 1942's, with no appearance changes, but with a number of new engineering features. Most of these came about as a result of lessons learned during the war. A new type of oil pump provided maximum oil pressure at low engine speeds—even at idle. New military-type housing vents were incorporated in the rear axles to provide a more positive seal against dirt and other foreign matter. A spring-loaded sealing-type vent opened automatically to relieve presure built up in the differential. The steering gear was improved and made heavier to provide longer life and greater ease in steering. The steering gear ratio was increased in half-ton models. Axle shafts were increased in diameter to provide longer life. Half-ton and one-ton models had a new four-pinion differential in place of the old two-pinion type.

Job-Rated Era Engines					
For half-ton trucks					
Year	Bore x Stroke	CID	BHP	Torque	Compression
1939	3 1/8 x 4 3/8	201.3	70 @ 3000	148lb/ft	6.7
1940	3 1/8 x 4 3/8	201.3	79 @ 3000	154lb/ft	6.7
1941	3 1/8 x 4 3/8	201.3	82.5 @ 3000	160lb/ft	6.7
For three-quarter-ton and one-ton trucks					
1939	3 1/4 x 4 3/8	217.76	77 @ 3000	158lb/ft	6.5
1940	3 1/4 x 4 3/8	217.76	82 @ 3000	166lb/ft	6.5
1941	3 1/4 x 4 3/8	217.76	85 @ 3000	170lb/ft	6.5
For half-ton and three-quarter-ton trucks					
1942-1947	3 1/4 x 4 3/8	217.76	95 @ 3600	172lb/ft	6.6
For one-ton trucks					
1942-1947	3 1/4 x 4 7/8	230.2	102 @ 3600	184lb/ft	6.7

Chapter 5

Pilot House Era Trucks1948-1953

★★★★	1948-1953 Half-ton pickup
★★★	1948-1953 Half-ton panel
★★	1948-1953 Three-quarter- and one-ton pickup
★★	1948-1953 Three-quarter- and one-ton stake and platform
★★★★★	1948-1953 Half-ton Spring Special pickup
★★	1949-1953 One-ton Route Van

From the most popular era we now move to the second most popular, the Pilot House Era of 1948-1953. *Pilot House* was chosen for the name of this era because it so aptly describes the new cab design that is one of its hallmarks. Several other titles could have been chosen because there is so much to be said about the distinctive new trucks Dodge introduced to an admiring public in 1948.

Innovative Era would have been another excellent choice, because these new Dodge trucks were innovative in a number of ways that will be ex-

panded on later in this chapter. Another title that has a very catchy ring to it is *Practical Pickups Era*. The rational behind this title will be evident, too, in the following pages. The final possible title for this era is simply the *B-Series Era*, since this is the first era in which the entire series shared the same letter designation. The preceeding era, however, came close. The letter designation for the first year of the Job-Rated Era was the T-Series, the following year it changed to V-Series, and for the balance of its run it was the W-Series. It is common now to refer

A 1948 three-quarter-ton stake with standard cab.

A 1948 half-ton pickup (express) with standard cab. The cargo box, running boards, and rear fenders painted black was the standard paint scheme for pickups during the entire Pilot House Era.

to all years of the Job-Rated Era as simply the W-Series. Series means all the model years in which the same basic chassis and cab continue as is, albeit with yearly mechanical and/or appearance updates and improvements. A logical practice that began with the B-Series, or Pilot House Era, is that in every year in which a significant change in either mechanical or appearance changes were made, the suffix number changed. For example,

B-1 is for the years 1948 and 1949; B-2 is for 1950, at which time several mechanical updates were made; B-3 is for 1951 and 1952 for the appearance changes made in 1951; B-4 is for 1953, at which time both appearance and mechanical advancements appeared.

Many Dodge truck enthusiasts believe the Pilot House Era trucks were the smartest-looking and the most expertly engineered trucks in Dodge

Wouldn't it be nice to be able to buy an original low-mileage 1947 panel for $995? It is probably the second truck from the right. The third truck from the right is a 1945 panel. The pickup on the far left is a 1946 or 1947 half-ton, and the pickup to its right is a 1948-1950 half-ton.

This original-condition 1948 B-1-B half-ton, standard-cab pickup is owned by Don and Becky Evans of Bakersfield, California.

Len Marconi of Kingston, Pennsylvania, is the owner of this superb B-1 half-ton woody wagon. These trucks are very desirable and are extremely rare.

history. Modern appearance and modern engineering advancements were the goals of Dodge engineers for these trucks. Did they succeed? The following pages will answer that question.

We will examine the new Pilot House Era trucks in some detail, from a number of different points of view, including a discussion of the trucks' chassis, driveline, cab, front-end sheet metal, bodies, and model lineup. As this era unfolds, the collector will see dramatic changes in just six short years. Dodge trucks quickly evolved from a forties-type work-only pickup in 1948 to the modern, innovative, and up-to-date dual-use pickup fielded in 1953. All this within the same basic series. Let's pick this new pickup apart, starting from the bottom, with its chassis, to see why it was so innovative and practical.

Chassis

For starters, the Pilot House Era's chassis sported a new, rugged frame with shorter wheelbases for all models. Dodge engineers shortened wheelbases for two reasons. Moving the front axle back 6in, while the engine was moved forward, placed more of the truck's load on the front wheels to provide better weight distribution.

Second, easier handling and driving were introduced with the shorter wheelbase and wider front tread width, together with cross steering, another new feature of the Pilot House Era. Cross steering permitted a full 37-degree turning angle to the left or right. The new Dodge trucks could be turned in much smaller circles—a decided advantage in backing and maneuvering in busy traffic and other working situations. Another advantage of cross steering is that it greatly reduced road shock through the steering wheel.

Driveline

The Pilot House Era trucks were not what we could call "new from the wheels up," but nevertheless they represented a revolutionary change from the Job-Rated Era trucks. The only area of consequence that didn't change was the driveline. Engines, for example, carried over without any change. But just hold on: In 1950 and again in 1953 major driveline innovations chalked up two more Dodge industry firsts. More on them later.

Cab

Dodge engineering's goal in designing this new cab was to provide for total driver comfort and utility. Highlighted throughout the new cab were utility, ease of maintenance, strength, maneuverability, and driver comfort. Many drivers had requested a truly comfortable cab, and Dodge engineers answered with a cab that was higher, wider, and longer. It was also fully weatherproofed, provided excellent vision and clear floor space, a large fixed windshield, a form-styled adjustable seat, and a neat appearance.

One would expect to find significant cab improvements in the Pilot House Era because the very name suggests cab improvements. As a matter of fact, the new standard, deluxe, and custom cabs provided more room, more visibility, more safety, and more comfort for the driver. The roomy new cab was 6 3/8in wider, 2 1/2in higher, and 3in longer. Three large men could ride in it without crowding. The patented Chrysler Corporation's chair-height seats gave plenty of leg support under the knees and could be adjusted 7in forward and backward. Dodge engineers had totally redesigned the seat's platform so that it now rode on a tubular frame mounted on ball bearing rollers. Entrance to the cab was enhanced, too, through wider and higher doors equipped with hold-open checks. The back cushion was also adjustable for maximum comfort. For added comfort, the seat cushion rode on air (an innovation called "Air-O-Ride") as well as on steel coil springs. A convenient hand control allowed the driver to adjust cushion buoyance to suit his weight or to road conditions.

Drivers appreciated the any-season, any-weather comfort built into the new cab by an all-weather heating and cooling system. A fresh air intake system placed behind the grille brought outside air into the cab either directly or through the heater defroster system. Vent wings in the side windows and a larger cowl ventilator also brought in cooling fresh air.

Dodge drivers "sat on top of the world" on their chair-height seats, or so it seemed, because of the new "360-degree vision" afforded in the Pilot House cabs. The cab was attached to the chassis on four soft rubber mountings for the benefit of the driver. Driver vision was tremendously increased through new windshields, which were higher by 3in and wider by 4in. For the first time since 1933, the windshields were the fixed type, not the ventilating or crank-open type. Side glass was also proportionately higher and wider, too. And on deluxe and custom cabs, the cab corner blind spot was eliminated by the use of new, curved-corner windows, a very welcome safety feature.

Ease of Servicing

Carried forward from the Job-Rated Era was the ability to completely service these new trucks from the left side. The gas filler, oil filler, radiator, battery, generator oiling, distributor service, fan belt adjustment, brake master cylinder, and voltage regulator were all located on the left side. The gas tank was safely located inside the left frame rail below the driver's seat.

Cab Interior

Dodge designers for several years had been concerned with driver comfort, safety, and productivity, and the Pilot House Era continued the trend. The cab interior was again fully lined and also had thick insulation on the firewall to reduce engine heat and noise. The all-new instrument panel was both attractive and functional. A large, easy-to-read speedometer was placed directly in front of the driver, and all other gauges were positioned in a line to its right. The instrument panel was engineered so instruments could be removed from the

Dodge management sent a fleet of its new fluid-drive-equipped light duties around the country in July 1950. The sign on the doors says, "New Fluid Drive only on Dodge Job-Rated Trucks." The sign on the cargo box reads, "Try a demonstration now!" The first truck is a three-quarter-ton, the second a half-ton, and the third a one-ton.

front of the panel. For the driver's pleasure, the instrument panel was designed to accept a radio as an optional item, with a speaker grille standard. Other accessories engineered into the new cab for the driver's convenience and comfort included an ashtray, cigar lighter, dual electric windshield wipers, armrests, dome light, and vent windows. A natural benefit from moving the engine forward was the fact that the gear shift lever also moved forward, which resulted in more leg and foot room for a helper sitting in the center of the seat. It also made it easier for the driver to slide across the seat

This photo was taken early in January 1948, shortly after production of Pilot House Era trucks began.

The Rare 1949-1955 Dodge Route Van

The Route Van may be the Pilot House Era's least-known truck. When was the last time you saw a Route Van—either in service, quietly parked and retired, in a salvage yard, at a truck show—anywhere? I only know of three Route Vans. One in New England is used to sell ice cream at car shows; a second is in Portland, Oregon, and the third—a 1952 in fair original condition—was recently spotted in Mankato, Minnesota.

The Route Van is a shining example of a great idea—on paper. But when the idea was executed, the final product was sadly lacking. For example, the Route Van was overengineered and overbuilt to the point where its price made it uncompetitive. It also suffered from quality problems, including poor body structural integrity. Its body and side and rear doors rattled and squeaked because of a shortage of bracing and strengthening.

Another major design flaw? The gas tank sat directly in front of the driver and immediately beside the engine, with the gas tank filler located at the front of the truck! I shudder to think what would happen in the event of a front-end crash. The Route Van originally was to be a stand-drive truck. Too late, Dodge discovered that Divco already had all the rights to stand-drive sewn up.

Dodge management had such high hopes for the truck they built a special plant exclusively for Route Vans adjacent to the main truck plant. The truck's sales volume never justified this expense. Dodge later built military trucks for the Korean War on the Route Van's line. It's doubtful Dodge could have justified the Route Van program's cost even if it had captured the lion's share of the market, since that market in those days only amounted to 15,000-20,000 units per year.

Still, this least-known Pilot House Era truck merits an in-depth look. The primary design goal was to substantially lower the truck floor's height since a low floor was important in reducing driver fatigue. To accomplish this, two rear axles were used. The load-supporting axle was the usual, rugged, I-beam type. The axle that moved the load was an important engineering advancement. It made possible a tremendous frame kick-up, which lowered the floor 10in closer to the ground than any other delivery truck. When the Route Van was parked at the curb, the driver had to extend his leg only a few inches—half the normal distance—to reach the ground.

Route Vans were built on three wheelbase lengths: 102, 117, and 142in. The one-ton Route Van seen here has the 102in wheelbase.

Two windshield wipers were standard. The Route Van was the world's first truck equipped with fluid drive.

The low floor height was only one of several unique and innovative ways Dodge engineers tried to design a truck that would increase driver efficiency. They also moved the engine far to the right to provide more sitting and driving space for the driver and to allow unobstructed access to the cargo area. The space over the engine was turned into a convenient package shelf. Extra-wide doors at the front and rear allowed the driver to walk straight in or out with his arms full of packages without twisting or turning sideways.

The interior height at the center was 6ft, 4in, providing plenty of head room for most men to move around comfortably, and the "nonslip" safety steel floor was flat, making it very easy for the driver to "work" his load. Even though the Route Van was unusually high inside, it had a low center of gravity, giving the truck good stability and a good ride.

Routine servicing was accomplished either through an outside front-opening hood or an inside hinged engine cover. The front-opening hood gave access to the radiator, gas tank filler, oil level gauge, and oil filler pipe. All other engine servicing was done through the inside engine cover.

Another innovative and unique feature introduced in the Route Van was fluid drive, which was not available on other light-duty Dodge trucks until 1950. A Route Van with fluid drive was also equipped with an electro-hydraulic holder system for the rear service brakes. The driver had only to flick a switch on the steering column cowl bracket to apply the service brakes, that is, as a parking brake. When he returned, he flicked the switch to "off," kicked the brake pedal, and drove off.

The combination of fluid drive with the electro-hydraulic brake system improved driver efficiency greatly. For example, the driver could shift into his driving gear when first starting out and not shift again for the balance of his route. Instead, he could set his electric switch upon stopping, letting the fluid drive "slippage" idle his engine, flick off the electric brake upon returning, and simply press the accelerator pedal to drive off.

While I do not have production figures for Route Vans, I suspect production was very low since delivery trucks were not a significant part of the total truck business and quite a number of companies competed in this small market segment. The Route Van's price also tended to dampen sales.

Route Vans stayed in production, basically unchanged, through the 1955 model year. To Dodge's credit, engineers did move the gas tank to the rear of the Route Van later in its production run.

to exit from the right door. As a safety measure, only the right side door could be locked from the outside.

Front-End Sheet Metal

It was the appearance of these new Pilot House Era trucks, with their smoothly flowing lines, that set them apart from other new trucks more than any other feature. The trucks debuted in January 1948, by the way, which was about the same time Ford's Bonus Built trucks appeared, and a few months after Chevrolet's Advanced Design models came on the market. One magazine writer at the time said that the new Dodge trucks had "advanced type styling." Dodge's styling was in fact advanced; Chevrolet's new trucks were advanced for them but were not really "Advanced Design." Dodge's most prominent styling feature was the new, larger, true three-man cab, as discussed above, with fender-through-door styling. That term means that the front fenders were not a bolted-on item, as was the practice with all other makes; rather, the front fenders were now integrated with other front-end sheet metal and made as

wide as the cab. This is now the accepted style and common to the entire industry. Another design element that not only added to this truck's appearance but also to its Practical Pickups reputation was the new, simple styling and construction of the

A 1948 half-ton panel with deluxe cab, as seen by the vent wings in cab doors.

The man seen here has just taken his early twenties Dodge Brothers screenside into a Dodge dealer to trade it in for a 1948 half-ton pickup. The screenside was still in daily use.

rear fenders. They were a cycle-style fender, bolted on for easy removal and for low-cost repair in the event of damage. Their simple, half-round design balanced beautifully with the front fender's wheel opening. This was the last new Dodge truck series designed with the Ram hood ornament as a standard feature, until the early eighties, when the ornament was reintroduced. The four attractive horizontal grille bars were standard in stainless on light-duty models and painted on larger trucks.

Dodge engineers stayed with the side-opening hood for the Pilot House trucks to make the back of the engine as easy to service as the front of the engine.

Pickup Bodies

We now come to the one new feature that, more than any other new feature, shows why we considered designating these trucks the "Innovative Pickups" or the "Practical Pickups": the new cargo box. It added to the outstanding appearance of these pickups. Dodge reengineered and redesigned the cargo box to increase its size for more load-carrying capacity, greater strength, and an improved appearance. This may sound simple and logical, but nevertheless, the new pickup body was a big leap forward in pickup design. After all, pickups are intended to be used for hauling. Then why

not make them more capable of doing their job? That's exactly what the new Dodge pickups delivered.

When was the last time you saw a low-side cargo box on a modern pickup? In keeping with the practical nature of Dodge engineers, the new cargo box was simply called a "high-side." No marketer's fancy jargon here. Length did not change, but the width of a half-ton's cargo box increased by .75in and by 5.75in on three-quarter-ton and one-ton pickups. The flare boards and tailgate on all models were 5.5in higher. The floor was built using oak boards with steel skid strips. Load capacity for the half-ton pickup increased by 34 percent, and the load capacity of three-quarter-ton and one-ton pickups increased by an enormous 48 percent!

Panel Body

The new panel was much improved in construction and style. It was larger, with a new, smooth surface design that added to its appearance. A solid steel roof replaced the former soft insert type. The floor at the front end was flush with the cab's floor and had shaped skid strips welded to the subfloor replacing the former flat, bolted-on skid strips to improve sealing against dust and dirt. The new rear doors were exceptionally high and had improved sponge rubber sealing. The load space was 85in long by 62in wide and almost 55in high, giving a capacity of 155cu-ft.

Model Lineup

The Pilot House Era's model lineup reflected the changes occurring in the nation's economy. Absent from the lineup was the canopy, which no longer served an important economic purpose. The panel was only available as a half-ton. Stake and platform models could be ordered on three-quarter-ton (7.5ft) and one-ton chassis (7.5ft and 9ft), with two wheelbase lengths for one-ton models. Pickups, of course, were available in three sizes: half-ton (6.5ft), three-quarter-ton (7.5ft), and one-ton (7.5ft and 9ft).

Mechanical Improvements

We tend to remember the wholesale changes in the 1948 and 1949 trucks' cab styling, front sheet metal, and cargo boxes, but not many mechanical improvements stand out in our memories. And this is basically true. While mechanical improvements were made, they really were minor refinements and fine tuning. There were a whole host of these, but we will not get into all the details. Suffice it to say that mechanical improvements ranged all the way from mounting the coil on the engine instead of on the firewall, to providing huskier batteries. The entire list of such refinements would be several pages long, but none of the changes was of major significance.

1950

An excellent way to gauge whether significant change took place in the Dodge truck line is to learn, "Did the series designation change?" And so it did in 1950—from B-1 to B-2. This time the changes were of a mechanical nature. The most important changes benefited the driver.

In the spirit of accuracy, which is an important consideration for the collector, there is an issue that must be brought to light at this time. That nagging feeling of seeing physical evidence that doesn't always square with what you read tends to be a burr under your saddle. So, not to split hairs, but in order to set the record straight for those who need to know, we should note that there was an intermediate B-1 model before the B-2s came into being. There may be collectors out there who have 1949 model trucks with a three-speed shift lever on the column who question whether their truck is really a 1949 or 1950 model. The following will give them peace:

The intermediate model was built between August 1, 1949, and October 1, 1949, and it was the same as the B-2s, which superseded them begin-

The 1948 Dodge one-ton pickup carried a man-size 9ft cargo box.

ning in October 1, 1949. These trucks were identified by the letter "X" stamped immediately after the serial number on both the frame side rail and the serial number plate.

Let me make this clear, as it is quite simple. The B-2 models were reengineered, and when ready, they were released for production without waiting for a new model year. Putting a new idea into production at the time it was available was something Dodge engineers had done for many years, beginning way back in the original Dodge Brothers Company days.

Steering Column Shift Lever

The first change for all low-tonnage trucks was a three-speed transmission shift lever mounted on the steering column. When combined with the new "right spot" hand-pull emergency brake lever, that change translated into an uncluttered

Ron Ashley of Prineville, Oregon, has owned this 1949 one-ton stake since 1956. It has not been restored; rather, it is an all-original truck except for tires and muffler. Ron says he drives it every day.

The US Navy purchased a large quantity of these 1950 half-ton low-side pickups. Note the nonstandard reflectors on its tailgate and the inside rearview mirror. The low-side box was new for 1950.

floor, free from all handles and levers. Drivers and passengers could move from one side of the cab to the other without bumping into any obstructions. The right spot emergency brake lever located the handle under the dash just to the right of the driver and angled it conveniently toward him to make it easy to grab and pull. A ratchet device held it in place when set. A simple counterclockwise half-turn released the brake, and a spring pulled it back to its off position.

A deluxe cab 1952 half-ton panel. The front appearance of trucks of the Pilot House Era changed in 1951. The only clues to distinguish a 1951 from a 1952 are subtle. In 1951 the medallion in the center of the grille was chrome, while in 1952 it was painted argent. And in 1951 the headlight rims were chrome-plated, while in 1952 they were painted black.

Low-Side Pickup Cargo Box

I am not so sure what to call the third major change incorporated at new model introduction time. This change was a low-side cargo box for half-ton pickups. In size and appearance, it was the same as the cargo box from the Job-Rated Era. The low-side was the standard cargo box, and the high-

Milt Smazik of Illinois owns this 1951 B-3-B half-ton. Note the aftermarket grille guard and right side spare tire carrier.

The US Post Office purchased these Dodge half-ton panels in 1952. It was unusual for a truck to be equipped with turn signals at the factory in 1952.

side was an extra-cost option. The low-side was not capable of carrying as big a load as the high-side, and it looked out of scale with the rest of the truck, which had been designed for the high-side cargo box. This probably explains why one sees very few of them. They are not recommended to the collector. Even though they are admittedly rare, they are not desirable. The low-side cargo box was a dumb idea.

Fluid Drive

The last major mechanical improvement for 1950 was a late-in-the-year addition. Fluid drive was available only for the Route Van back in 1949, and it proved so successful that engineering expanded its use to all light-duty trucks.

This is definitely an option the collector should look for. Fluid drive gives some of the advantages of an automatic transmission and is absolutely easier to drive and works like a charm. With fluid drive one could speed along in high, then creep along in heavy traffic, and then speed up again, all without touching the gearshift lever or clutch. If you drive a truck equipped with fluid drive without a load, you can start off in high gear and stay in high gear—except for reverse—for long periods of time. Your getaways will not be like a jackrabbit, but you sure save a lot of shifting.

Fluid drive is really handy for cornering. You can slow the truck without stopping, then, when you have completed your turn, you simply step on the gas, and it accelerates with no jerking or jumping. If you stop on a hill, you can prevent rolling backwards simply by stepping on the gas just a bit. The only change as far as the cab interior is that with a four-speed transmission and fluid drive the shift lever is located further back on the floor to compensate for the length of the fluid drive unit, which is located between the engine and the transmission. Fluid drive is simple and absolutely trouble free.

1951 and 1952

The 1951 and 1952 models were designated the B-3 Series. This tells us right off that considerable changes had been made from 1950. We have an interesting pattern developing here. In 1948 and 1949, changes were more cosmetic than mechanical. In 1950, the major changes were mechanical, not related to appearance. And in 1951, the major changes were again mostly to appearance. Not that Dodge engineers ever slowed down in making mechanical improvements; they did make a number of improvements in the 1951 models that made them better-quality trucks and enabled them to work harder and longer. But nevertheless, 1951 was a year of styling changes.

New Front End Styling

Whether or not you believe that 1951's styling was an improvement is a matter of personal taste. Dodge designers thought it was an improvement, but I don't see any evidence that it is preferred by collectors, because more B-1 and B-2 pickups are owned by collectors than are B-3 and B-4 series pickups. The new grille was formed by two large horizontal louvers with a Job-Rated medallion placed in the center of the grille. The best and easiest way to distinguish a 1951 model from a 1952 model is by this medallion. Only in 1951 was the medallion chrome plated; in 1952 it was painted argent. The only other way to distinguish a 1952 from a 1951: The headlight rims in 1951 were chrome plated, while in 1952 they were painted black. This change was made because of the need for chrome to fight the Korean War.

Other new styling features included a redesigned front bumper; new grille guards (actually the same as before, but now only two were used instead of three); 4in diameter parking lights; and a new Dodge nameplate centered directly above the grille. The Dodge Ram hood ornament was an extra-cost option.

Cab Improvements

The instrument panel was restyled in a modern manner with all of the instruments located directly in front of the driver. A new cluster on the right housed the radio speaker grille and optional ashtray and cigar lighter. These two options are

This 1951 half-ton pickup is about as well-equipped as a 1951 Dodge pickup could be. It has the deluxe cab, fluid drive, front bumper guards, a rear bumper, and chrome grille bars. Chrome grille bars were an option only in 1951.

A Very Special Truck:
A Dodge 1953 Spring Special

The Dodge half-ton Spring Special was a Pilot House Era marketing tool used to increase pick-up business after the winter sales doldrums. To this day, Chrysler Corporation continues to run Spring Specials of various types in both car and truck lines. A 1953 Spring Special was a half-ton pickup painted with an attractive and distinctive two-tone paint combination. Hardly anyone remembers them since they were not sold in great quantities and few have survived. I know of the existence of only one other Spring Special, which just happens to be another 1953 model. In all my research on Dodge trucks over a span of many years, I have found only one piece of literature (in the Detroit Public Library's Automotive History Collection) that mentions a 1948-1953 Spring Special.

This 1953 Dodge half-ton Spring Special is owned and was restored by Val and Beverly Weakley of Greenwood, Indiana. It is a very special truck indeed, and Bev and Val have an interesting story to tell.

Val remembered seeing Spring Specials when he was a boy, was impressed by their unique paint schemes, and decided he wanted to make a Spring Special of his own. Gerald Seacat, Val's business partner's father, owned a Dodge and Plymouth dealership in Milltown, Indiana, in the early fifties. Val chose an early fifties Dodge pickup to restore because he preferred a Dodge for its bigger three-man cab and side-opening (butterfly-type) hood.

He purchased a very rough but authentic 1953 Spring Special that sported an incorrect front clip from an earlier truck, and a 1953 half-ton (with a Truck-O-Matic, or TOM) that had been left in a wet woods for twenty-one years;

Gerald's dad had sold the truck when it was new. It was very rough, and offered little for salvage except the TOM and the instrument panel knobs. Val bought a third truck, a 1952, from an Indianapolis area salvage yard for its correct front sheet metal. Finally, Val traded the frame from the 1953 TOM to Gerald's brother for a complete 1951 pickup with decent sheet metal.

Val began the restoration process in 1989 by disassembling all four trucks. From this mountain of parts he chose the best frames, three cabs, three sets of doors, two sets of front fenders, and one pickup body, and sent them to Redi-Strip. His original plan was to make two pickups from four, but after the disassembly and stripping, it was apparent that there were only enough good parts to build one truck.

He bought NOS (new old stock) rear fenders from a local Dodge dealer because the rear fenders of a 1953 pickup are the same as those for 1985 models.

The cargo box's headboard and tailgate were modified from new old stock (NOS) parts. These NOS parts, however, were for modern cargo boxes, which are 4in wider than the 1953's cargo box. So they had to be cut down, a very tricky job indeed. The NOS tailgate did

A cab interior view of the 1953 Spring Special gives one a better indication of the detail with which it was restored.

Val and Beverly Weakley's exceptional 1953 Spring Special. It is painted two shades of blue.

not have the Dodge name embossed into it as the tailgate did in 1953, so the old tailgate's embossed name was cut out and welded into place on the NOS tailgate.

A skilled craftsman made the best sheet metal parts good-as-new by welding in metal patches and expertly finishing them.

The engine was rebuilt, the brakes were revived with NOS parts, and the TOM was torn down, carefully inspected, reassembled, and refilled with new 10-weight motor oil. (It ended up working perfectly later.) The special carburetor, as well as all other TOM fittings, were taken from the original truck; all of these parts were later replaced by NOS parts. The exhaust manifold was split, and dual mufflers and tail pipes were installed. Dual exhausts can correctly be called an option for trucks of this vintage because dealers in the early fifties routinely did this work on customers' trucks.

NOS parts replaced all the original rubber parts, nameplates, hubcaps, beauty rings, headlight rims, interior door handles, and several other small mechanical and trim items. Every nut and bolt, washer, belt, hose, and bracket, the wood in the cargo box and the skid strip and hanger were replaced with new parts. So were the paint, wiring harness, upholstery, glass, and even the rivets from the spring hangers.

This shot of a 1953 Dodge half-ton Spring Special is one of less than a handful of Chrysler photos existing of 1948-1953 Spring Specials. Spring Specials are among the most prized of all collectible Dodge pickups.

There isn't one part or piece on this truck, no matter how small, that wasn't remade or replaced. Val and Beverly spent $16,000 out of pocket on their restoration, and this does not take Val's time into consideration.

To preserve its newness, Weakley's Spring Special is trailered to shows, where it is displayed under a portable tent. In the year since its restoration was completed, the truck has only logged twenty-one miles!

---

quite rare. Owners of 1951-1953 Dodge trucks should try to find these options because they add a lot of interest to a truck's instrument panel. The cab interior now took on a two-tone effect with a light tan roof and quarter panels contrasting with rich brown seat upholstery. All of the cab's hardware, such as door handles and window regulators, were given a modern touch by Dodge designers.

Driver Comfort

The new seat was much more comfortable due mostly to a thicker seat pad cushion. Even more important was that the seat back contour was redesigned to better fit the driver's back. Although not an improvement as far as comfort was concerned, the seat cushions were now trimmed with welts to give them a neater, trimmer, and more finished look.

To make the new Dodge trucks easier to drive and more comfortable, the steering wheel was moved down and back. This improvement added considerably to driveability. A collector should seriously consider a 1951, 1952, or 1953 model Dodge. These improvements to driver comfort, when added to the shorter wheelbases and cross

steering of these models, make them very responsive and highly maneuverable. Pilot House trucks are a real treat to drive.

Oriflow Shock Absorbers

One final improvement for the driver's benefit was the addition of Chrysler's "oriflow" shock absorbers. These shocks provided new standards of riding comfort and driving ease for trucks. They assured a really smooth ride on even rough roads. Oriflow shocks differed from ordinary shocks in that oriflows made new use of hydraulic principles. The flow of fluid in ordinary shocks was controlled by spring-loaded valves. Oriflows, on the other hand, used pistons with long fluid passages and no valves. Thus, the action of oriflow shocks was infinitely variable, successfully controlling the ride on any kind of bumpy road. Chrysler used the same shocks on all of its passenger cars.

The Universal Vehicle

Beginning in 1947, Dodge Truck published a quarterly magazine for buyers of new Dodge trucks called *The Job-Rater*. The issue for the second quarter of 1951 carried a very interesting article. It is the earliest publication I have ever found that talks about the pickup as a dual-use vehicle—that is, serving both as the family car and as a commercial vehicle. The article used the terms *versatile pickup* and *universal vehicle* to describe the pickup's dual functions.

The article pointed out two key advantages that put Dodge at the forefront of this market. The first was fluid drive, which was without any argument a Dodge exclusive. The article said, "Surprising to dealers who sell both cars and trucks is the way the vehicle is 'catching on' with women—especially since the advent of gyrol fluid drive for trucks. Women residing on farms and ranches prefer this new type of vehicle to any other means of transportation for shopping in town. They find it just as easy to drive as a passenger car. And, for some of them there seems to be a new thrill of achievement attached to driving a truck."

This logic is easy to follow because a pickup equipped with fluid drive and a three-speed transmission with the shift lever located on the steering column had in reality the same drive train as a Dodge passenger car. The pickup afforded the woman driver a higher seat and, in Dodge's Pilot House cab, superior visibility. The pickup was easier to handle, too, with its short wheelbase and cross steering. A farmer's wife could haul more groceries in the pickup, too.

The second reason the article suggested for the popularity of pickups with women drivers was the fact that numerous accessories were now available to make driving more pleasurable. Some examples would be the fresh air heater system, radio, adjustable seat, fully lined interior, ashtray, turn signals, and custom cab equipment. Custom cab features included door vent windows, rear quarter windows, dome light, armrest, dual sun visors, foam rubber seat padding, deluxe seat back, cowl ventilator, and dual electric windshield wipers.

Mechanical Updates

Mechanical improvements for 1951 fill another list several pages in length. Some highlights the collector should look for include: higher compression ratios on both light-duty engines; narrow fan belt and new type water bypass for all light-duty trucks; four-speed syncromesh transmission in

This closeup photo of the front of a 1953 half-ton pickup clearly details styling changes for 1953: new rear fenders, hubcaps, Dodge nameplate above the grille, absence of striping on the grille bars, and chrome headlight and parking light rims. Note also the "Truck-O-Matic" nameplate on the side of its hood.

This former fire truck had only 2,828mi on its clock when it went on sale nine years ago. All the fire equipment—lights, sirens, etc.—were included. What a wonderful find for the collector.

What is special about this 1948 or 1949 116in wheelbase one-ton chassis cab cannot be seen. It was one of a number of specials built for AT&T. It was equipped with fluid drive, a T-137 transfer case, 4WD, and a special fuel tank (the only special that can be seen). The collector should be aware that Dodge engineers authorized specials of all types. You might find a rare Dodge sometime and be confused if you didn't know that specials were common.

place of spur type; bigger king pins; turning angle increased from 37 to 39 degrees; horn ring made standard on all light-duty models; and windshield wiper pivots moved outward from the center to provide more useable wiping surface.

Other mechanical improvements were made for 1952. One change that collectors should note is that the front wheel brake cylinders for 1952 were changed to the straight bore-type from the previous stepped-type. This is useful information for the owner who has to replace the front brake wheel cylinders on his or her truck. Don't allow the counter person to send you home with the wrong part.

Model Lineup

No changes except that a low-side cargo box was made standard for all pickups: half-, three-quarter-, and one-ton models.

1953

The 1953 Dodge pickups were distinctive in both their pleasing new appearance and in mechanical improvements that contributed to driveability. First let's talk about the most obvious—those we can readily see. New streamlined rear fenders on all pickups are the first changes noticed. They are the same fenders that Dodge used on its fender-side pickups, or (as they would be called in a few more years) Utiline model pickups, into the 1985 model year.

At the front of the truck was a new elongated Dodge nameplate above the grille bars. Paint striping on the grille bars was deleted. The final change

was that the headlight and parking light rims were chrome plated because the Korean War had slowed down, and supplies were not so strained.

Cab Interior

The cab interior was made even more attractive since it was trimmed in two-tone colors of maroon and grey. The door trim panels were edged with a plastic binding of contrasting color.

The seat cushion was permanently related to the back cushion and was attached on the tubular seat frame by sturdy clips. The peg-type adjustment to the angle of the seat's backrest was eliminated.

For the first time ever a Dodge nameplate was mounted in the center of the instrument panel. The nameplate replaced a former decorative chrome strip.

Panel

Two changes of note were made to the panel. First, the panel's floor was changed to two pieces

Pilot House Era Engines					
For half- and three-quarter-ton trucks					
Year	Bore x Stroke	CID	BHP	Torque	Compression
1948-1949	3 1/4 x 4 3/8	217.76	95 @ 3600	172lb/ft	6.6
1950	3 1/4 x 4 3/8	217.76	96 @ 3600	172lb/ft	6.6
1951-1953	3 1/4 x 4 3/8	217.76	97 @ 3600	175lb/ft	7.0
For one-ton trucks					
1948-1949	3 1/4 x 4 7/8	230.2	102 @ 3600	184lb/ft	6.7
1950	3 1/4 x 4 7/8	230.2	102 @ 3600	187lb/ft	6.7
1951-1953	3 1/4 x 4 7/8	230.2	103 @ 3600	190lb/ft	7.0

of plywood with skip strips. Second, dual taillights became standard.

New Models

New models in 1953 were distinguished by changes to pickup cargo boxes more than anything else. After a futile try with low-side pickup bodies, Dodge management cut the low-side body back to the 108in wheelbase half-ton only.

Dodge's one new pickup model this year was a throwback to 1935's second series pickups. It was a 7.5ft pickup cargo box on a 116in-wheelbase half-ton chassis; a first for the big three. Offering half-ton pickups on two wheelbases with two cargo box lengths has become an industry standard still in use. This pickup was available with only the high-side box. The collector who wants an unusual and rare Dodge pickup should look for a 116in wheelbase half-ton 1953 pickup. I have never seen one.

M6 Automatic Transmission

Dodge engineers were not content with offering the industry's only cushioned drivetrain—that is, fluid drive. Now they shook up the industry by adding an automatic transmission. The smooth, certain, cushioned action of fluid drive had now proven itself in many thousands of trucks and in million of miles of tough truck service. It was time to move up to something even better.

"Truck-O-Matic," as Dodge marketing called it, was the same proven transmission used for many years in Dodge, DeSoto, and Chrysler pas-senger cars. In a passenger car it was called "Tip-Toe Shift." In reality it was a semiautomatic, not a true, full automatic. It required the use of a clutch to shift into gear (two forward ranges and reverse). Once in driving range, which was used for most driving, manual shifting was eliminated. The driver shifted up to high at the exact moment he wished by merely lifting his foot momentarily from the accelerator whenever the truck's speed exceeded 14mph. Downshifting into third was accomplished instantly by pushing the accelerator to the floor at speeds up to 40mph. Truck-O-Matic had four forward speeds—two in the power range and two in the driving range. Shifting up was easily accomplished with the accelerator pedal in either range. Shifting between power range and driving range was manually controlled.

With Truck-O-Matic, all normal starts were made in third gear. Bypassing first and second gears avoided high engine speeds, and wear on vital engine parts was reduced. This also meant less engine noise.

Truck-O-Matic was available only on half- and three-quarter-ton trucks. A fluid drive coupling was an integral element of Truck-O-Matic. Fluid drive continued as an option, too. Trucks equipped with Truck-O-Matic were identified by a nameplate attached to the bottom of the Dodge nameplate. The collector should seek a Truck-O-Matic-equipped truck. They are very rare; I know of only two. This transmission performs well and is trouble-free.

Miscellaneous Mechanical Improvements

As in every other year in the Pilot House Era, 1953 models had a number of miscellaneous mechanical improvements incorporated by Dodge engineers. A sample of a few related to light-duty models included a performance boost gained by raising the compression ratio of the 218 engine from 7.0 to 7.1. The exhaust pipe was now welded to the muffler. The emergency brake for half- and three-quarter-ton pickups equipped with fluid drive was increased 2in, bringing it to 7in. The Route Van's fuel tank was relocated to the rear of the frame; a high-output heater became an extra-cost option.

Chapter 6

V-8 Era Trucks 1954-1960

★★★	1954-1960 Half-ton pickup
★★★	1954-1960 Half-ton Town Panel
★★★	1955-1960 Half-ton Town Wagon
★★	1954-1960 Three-quarter- and one-ton pickup
★★	1954-1960 Three-quarter- and one-ton stake and platform
★★★★	1957-1960 Half-ton 4WD pickups
★★★	1958-1960 Three-quarter- and one-ton 4WD pickups
★★	1957-1960 Half-ton, three-quarter-, and one-ton 4WD stake and platform
★★★★	1957-1960 Half-ton 4WD Town Panel and Town Wagon
★★★★★	1957-1959 Half-ton Sweptside D100 pickup

Because 1954 marked the beginning of Dodge Truck's V-8 engine era, it can properly be said that the V-8 Era was a revolutionary era. After all, a truck's only purpose is to move a load—as big a load as possible, at the fastest practical speed, and at the lowest cost per mile. That is exactly what Dodge's lineup of V-8 engines delivered. Dodge's dependable "flathead" sixes were excellent engines and delivered economy and reliability for twenty-one years, but now it was time to deliver sparkling performance along with dependability.

New Design

Except for engines, the V-8 Era was one of evolutionary advancements. The Pilot House Era had been very successful because the new cab's outstanding styling and engineering innovations led to superior driver convenience, safety, and comfort. The V-8 Era's design built upon the lead- ership established during the Pilot House Era. Dodge's design experience and engineering know-how was perfectly manifested in the new V-8 Era's styling. The basic style motif of low, sleek lines presented a lower silhouette, which gave the appearance of exceptional width and massiveness. The

A 1954 half-ton pickup with special graphics was used to promote the first Dodge pickup with a V-8 engine.

This 1954 half-ton panel was on its way to Chicagoland. The sign on its door says, "A better deal for the man at the wheel. Dodge 'Job-Rated' trucks."

Four V-8 powered pickups were used to prove the speed, power, and durability of the all-new overhead valve 241ci V-8. This pickup is undergoing speed trials on the Bonneville Salt Flats.

pickup's overall height was reduced, as was the distance from the front fender to the top of the hood. Sloping the hood and revising the cab contours to eliminate sharp radii resulted in well-rounded and smooth lines.

The front-end sheet metal was completely new, with simplicity and serviceability the key notes. The pyramidally shaped grille opening, with

This rear view of a 1954 half-ton pickup on the left and a 1952 half-ton on the right clearly shows the 1954 pickup's lower height. The 1954 is a very rare Truck-O-Matic that belongs to Dan Schaffer of St Paul, Minnesota. The 1952 is owned by the author.

A high-line 1955 V-8-powered half-ton panel. Note its chrome full wheelcovers, wide whites, chrome bumpers, chrome grille guards, chrome rearview mirrors, chrome grille bars, chrome chevrons below the headlights, and Truck-O-Matic transmission.

two floating, heavy, horizontal grille bars, harmonized with the front fender and hood line for a very pleasing appearance without restricting the air flow to the radiator and engine for effective cooling. The grille bars were painted body color.

Six-cylinder models were identified by a Ram's Head medallion on the front. Eight-cylinder models were identified with a chrome V-8 emblem in place of the Ram's Head. For a dressier, upscale pickup, attractive brightmetal moldings at the center of each grille bar were available as extra-cost equipment. Small ornamental chrome chevrons located between the headlights and parking lights

This second series 1955 cab interior was typical of all models from 1954-1956.

completed the upscale look. Collectors who own this series of trucks should add these unique ornaments to their trucks for added interest.

Model Designations

Dodge truck engineers resisted using fenderside model designations for light-duty models, but did authorize their use for ton-and-a-half to four-ton trucks. Models were designated by a letter such as *F* for ton-and-a-half, *H* for two-ton, *T* for three-ton, and *Y* for four-ton trucks.

New Cab

The primary objectives of Dodge engineers for the new cab were comfort, safety, durability, and appearance. With these goals in mind, they created a cab that was completely new both in structure and in styling, inside and out, with a minimum of extraneous ornamentation.

Exterior styling shaped cab surfaces to present a smooth, well-rounded appearance. The front fender lines extended through the cab door surfaces and terminated with distinct definition at the rear of the cab. The idea was to provide distinct lines for two-tone paint combinations and well-defined areas that could be used as sign panels. The continuity of the front fender lines in combination with the lowered hood lines gave the impression of great length.

In order to make the driver's job both easier and safer, a large, one-piece curved windshield blended with the contour of the roof, and the increased vertical angularity of the windshield improved upward vision. For the first time since 1933, the interior windshield garnish moldings were eliminated, and a new, improved type of rubber seal was used.

Cab Structure

The cab underbody structure was reengineered totally to greatly reduce the total number of component pieces, facilitating assembly and service. The entire underbody was now a one-piece stamping. The dash and side toe-boards were one-piece stampings, too, welded to the underbody. With this new design, Dodge engineers created a

Thomas Traynor of Yorktown Heights, New York, had his truck photographed by a professional. Thomas bought his 1956 half-ton in 1979 and restored it in 1980. He and his wife enjoy driving and showing it only in the summer.

The 1954-1966 Dodge Town Panel and Town Wagon

Two trucks that are rapidly becoming more popular with collectors are Dodge's Town Panel and Town Wagon series of 1954-1966. Both models also became available as 4WD trucks in 1957.

In 1954, Dodge did not have a sedan delivery to compete with the popular Ford and Chevrolet models. Dodge's panel, which dated from 1948, received a major redesign in 1954 to make it look at home "on the boulevards." With its "sweptback exterior," the Town Panel, as it was now named, sported more attractive, modern, passenger-car styling to offer the customer a "sedan delivery vehicle" with the capacity of a full-size panel.

The Town Panel was offered in two trim levels to fit any job. With standard trim, it was a hard-working truck suited to tradesmen and others with tough jobs to do. With deluxe trim, it appealed to merchants in need of a prestigious boulevard delivery vehicle.

The 1954 Town Panel was built on a half-ton truck chassis with a 108in wheelbase and a 1,750lb payload rating. Powered by the dependable Dodge L-six 218ci engine, the Town Panel offered several transmissions: three-speed manual, three-speed manual with fluid drive, four-speed manual, or Truck-O-Matic.

Dodge's first light truck V-8 engine, the Power Dome, became available late in the 1954 model year. The Power Dome V-8 produced 145hp from a 241ci engine, the most powerful engine available in any light-duty truck, offering high road speeds, low fuel consumption, and exceptional acceleration.

In April 1955, Dodge launched the C-3 series, which remained unchanged through the 1956 model year. This series featured a new wraparound windshield for added visibility. The 218 was replaced with the 230, and the Power Dome V-8 was increased to 259. Buyers could for the first time order the three-speed Power-Flite, a fully automatic transmission, as an extra-cost option.

The Town Wagon, introduced later in the 1956 model year, combined rugged truck construction with passenger-car styling, comfort, and handling. The interior could hold either six passengers with room for 90cu-ft of cargo, or eight passengers and minimal cargo. All rear seats could be readily removed to convert the Town Wagon to a cargo hauler, and it had a 1,575lb payload capacity. Making these two beauties even more desirable, they were available with power brakes and power steering.

In 1957, the Town Panel and Town Wagon received "Forward Look Styling" with an all-new grille, forward-thrusting fenders, and hooded headlights. Since the early thirties, Dodge truck hoods had opened butterfly-style from the side. Dodge finally changed to a one-piece, alligator-type hood that could be opened a full 90 degrees for easier servicing. The Power Dome V-8 engine grew to 315ci, and a LoadFlite three-speed automatic transmission—controlled by convenient, dash-mounted, push-buttons—became an extra-cost option.

The first W100, "go-anywhere" 4WD Power Wagon versions of the Town Wagon and Town Panel became available in 1957 for customers needing a multiple-use workhorse (with a high ground clearance) to carry passengers, payloads, or both. Both Power Wagon

A very popular Dodge collectible is the half-ton Town Wagon series of 1955 to 1966. Shown here is a 1955 model.

models could have the L-6 or V-8 engines with three- or four-speed manual transmissions or the optional dash-mounted, push-button Load-Flite automatic (V-8 models only). An optional front-mounted 8,000lb winch added even more off-road ability.

1958 Power Wagons received an all-new hood and grille. The use of horizontal lines in the grille, wide-spaced dual headlights, and a new full-width hood made the front end bigger and broader. A redesigned front bumper wrapped around the fenders for added protection, and it added to the truck's lower, wider appearance. This style remained the same through 1966 (the last year of the series), with only a few minor changes.

The wheelbase stretched to 114in in 1961 to stay in line with other half-ton models. For 1961, the L-6 gave way to the modern overhead valve slant-six. This package then continued through 1966 with only minor yearly changes and improvements.

Dodge built the half-ton Town Wagon in both 2WD and 4WD versions. This one is a 2WD model. 4WD models are the most collectible.

cab with increased structural rigidity and improved sealing against dust, water, and air leaks.

The cab was mounted to the chassis at four points on rubber cushions. This eliminated noisy metal-to-metal contacts between cab and frame. It also provided flexibility to minimize sheet metal breakage and frame twist transmission to the cab. The mounting at the front on the steering-gear side was of hard rubber for greater steering-gear stability.

Visibility

The 1948-1953 Pilot House Era trucks were so named because of the superior visibility they offered in a cab that featured a greatly expanded glass area and a chair-height seat. Granted, the

A 1956 one-ton stake. One-ton stake trucks are increasing in popularity with collectors.

Pilot House Era was a giant step forward from the Job-Rated Era, and so was the V-8 Era another giant step forward in driver vision. Dodge engineers considered maximum visibility to be essential to driver safety, and therefore they substantially increased all glass areas.

By the use of a one-piece curved glass windshield, set in a very narrow rubber seal, and with corner pillars of the smallest practical size, the windshield glass area increased 8 percent.

Cab Door

To facilitate entry to the cab, the cab door was wider and higher than before. The increased opening width was achieved by relocating the hinge post forward to provide more room between the seat and the hinge post. Two hinges supported the door—a concealed one at the bottom and an exposed hinge at the top—which also provided a solid anchor for the rearview mirror.

Cab Seat

Dodge engineers had only one thought in mind when they designed the new chair-height seat for the V-8 Era pickup—driver comfort. Entirely new seat and back cushion contours gave the driver ideal knee position, correct posture back position, and proper eye-level position. The seat cushion was constructed of a two-stage-type spring designed to reduce rebound, with extra-heavy padding for a softer pillow. It was upholstered with two-tone gray, high-quality vinyl. Foam rubber seat cushions were standard equipment in the custom cab and available as extra-cost equipment in the standard cab.

The space under the seat was enclosed all around to provide an excellent storage place for tools and other equipment. The seat was adjustable on ball bearings, for 4in of fore and aft travel. A

Christopher Boles of Cottonwood, California, is the owner of this interesting 1956 half-ton. It is powered by a V-8 and has the PowerFlite fully automatic transmission with shift lever on the column.

large, easily operated seat release handle was placed at the bottom center of the seat frame within easy reach of the driver's hand.

Cab Trim

Larger, more stylish inside trim panels on the door in a two-tone dark gray that matched the seat upholstery were edged with an extruded vinyl in a contrasting light gray color to match the headlining.

A one-piece light gray headliner extended from the windshield over the roof to the top of the seat back, with separate side pieces above the cab doors. It presented an exceptionally neat appearance and made replacement simple and inexpensive. A full-formed black rubber floor mat fit smoothly over the entire floor.

Driver Comfort

Greater year-round driver comfort was provided by improving the air circulation within the cab for both slow- and fast-moving vehicles. This was accomplished in three ways:

1. Use of a cowl vent permitted fresh air into the cab without using the heater.

2. Cab door vent wings, which were standard equipment, permitted air into the cab as desired in foul weather when it was not desirable to lower the windows.

3. A factory-engineered fresh-air-type heater mounted high under the instrument panel left plenty of foot room. The heater was designed so that fresh air could be drawn into the cab and heated, or the air within the cab could be heated and recirculated. In warm weather the heater fan, now driven by a new, more powerful motor, could be used to draw cool air into the cab for slow-moving vehicles. The fresh-air intake admitted sufficient air by impact, without use of the fan, for faster moving vehicles.

Instrument Panel

The new instrument panel was a masterpiece of simplicity and utility. Two symmetrical oval insets, one at each end of the panel, provided the mountings for instruments and radio speaker. The insets made it easy for Dodge to convert the trucks to right-hand drive for the US Postal Service. There were also knockouts in the firewall and floor for the steering columns and pedals. For safety, the instrument panel had rounded contours at both top and bottom, eliminating any sharp edges or corners.

All control knobs and buttons were grouped together at the center of the instrument panel within easy reach of the driver. The glove box, located in the center of the instrument panel, was a brand new innovation for trucks. It was easily reached by the driver without stretching across the full width of the cab.

All instruments had subdued harmonious colors (white characters on black faces) and were located directly in front of the driver. They were indirectly lighted, making them clearly visible both day and night. Instruments were easily removed from the front for servicing.

Pickup Cargo Boxes

It is interesting to note that as late as 1954 an internal Dodge Truck engineering document referred to pickups as express trucks!

Pickup cargo boxes in the V-8 Era were the same as in the previous era in terms of style, lengths, widths, and heights. Low-side boxes were only offered for the half-ton models—both long and short.

A full-length running board between the back of the cab and rear fenders was a help in loading. Taillights were redesigned and incorporated plastic lenses with improved optics. Dual taillights were available for directional signals. The underslung-type spare-tire carrier was standard, but side-mounted spare-tire carriers were available at extra-cost. A step-type rear bumper was available at extra-cost for easier loading and for safety.

Six-Cylinder Engines

At new model introduction time, V-8 engines were only available on medium- and heavy-duty trucks. A light-duty V-8 was not ready for sale until in the spring. The old reliable 218 for half-ton and three-quarter-ton trucks returned in its familiar form. On the other hand, the 230 used in one-ton trucks, Power Wagons, and Route Vans was improved by increasing its power output. This was accomplished by increasing the compression ratio from 7.0 to 7.25, redesigning the manifold, and using a new camshaft with longer duration valve opening for better engine breathing.

Medium- and Heavy-Duty V-8s

We will only briefly mention these engines because they are outside the scope of this book. Two engines were used in medium- and heavy-duty trucks. Both were Hemis—the 241 for ton-and-a-half, two-ton, and two-and-a-half-ton trucks, and the huge 331 in two-and-three-quarter-ton to three-and-a-half-ton trucks. The enormous 413 L-6 was retained for the four-ton model. The powerful 331 Hemi was available in two forms (with single barrel or dual-barrel carbs), while the 241 was in every case equipped with a two-barrel carb. Gross horsepower in its double-barrel form jumped from 153

Bob and Hazel Seymour of Anchorage, Alaska, are the proud owners of this very nice late 1956 half-ton C-3-B pickup. It has a 116in wheelbase and is powered by a 269ci V-8. The Seymours have owned this truck since new and continue to drive it on nice days.

to 172, and gross torque went from 268 to a whopping 294. The double-barrel was a favorite with truckers all across America because this engine's exceptional performance surpassed that of every other gas truck on the nation's highways. The situation was much like what happened thirty-five years later, when Dodge engineers dropped the famous Cummins turbo diesel into three-quarter-ton and one-ton pickups.

An interesting fact about the Hemi engines was that they were actually a full 20 percent lighter than a six-cylinder engine of the same size! This in spite of the fact that the Hemi has a reputation as an exceptionally heavy V-8.

Light-Duty V-8

If you collect literature as part of your hobby interests, and I heartily recommend that you do, you should have a number of Dodge truck maga-

A 1955 one-ton with utility body was photographed on the street in Pine Island, Minnesota.

A 1957 Dodge V-8-powered D100 half-ton pickup compared to a 1957 GMC half-ton pickup.

zine articles in your collection. Truck magazines directed toward the truck enthusiast were not widely circulated before the late sixties to early seventies. Automobile articles for auto nuts date back to the end of World War II. Tom McCahill, who wrote automobile test articles for *Mechanics Illustrated*, was a favorite of mine in the early fifties.

In my file is an article from the November 1954 *Motor Trend* that is rather unusual because it deals with Dodge pickups, but in a rather backhanded way. The only reason the author wrote the article was that the 1954 Dodge pickup was powered by the same V-8 slated for 1955 Plymouths. If you remember those days, you know the whole

A 1957 Dodge half-ton minivan. This truck was originally built for the US Post Office. Dodge management thought so well of it that they made it available for the entire market.

country waited with bated breath to learn about the new V-8s soon to be introduced for Plymouth and Chevrolet cars. Most folks could have cared less about pickups in those days. The following quote gives a flavor for the times: "At presstime Don MacDonald called to ask if we'd like to have a driving impression of a Dodge truck. 'A truck!' I asked. 'What for?' 'It's got the new Plymouth engine.' 'By all means, then.' Two days later the following report came in the mail. 'Our usual activity,' began Don's comments, 'is not driving around in a pick-up truck. However, we just couldn't resist the offer of the Dodge half-ton for a week, especially since it gave us what amounts to a preview of the new Plymouth V8. 'We assume that most people who wheel trucks down the highway are getting paid for their time. If they happen to drive this commercialized hot rod, it's not a bad way to make a living. Comfort and driving ease are close to passenger car standards while performance (within speed limits) is actually better than most. Granted, Dodge put this optional 145-horsepower V8 in their lightest truck so that it would lug heavier loads up steeper hills more quickly. Still, it's nice, innocent fun to show your tailgate to competitors on any or all occasions. Many a plumber and plasterer in a Chevy or Ford was surprised to see our pick-up out-pick-up theirs, as well as continue on to the next stoplight more nimbly than the bulk of the carriage trade. The engine, geared to a 4.1 rear end, was smooth at all speeds and quiet as could be expected in non-insulated quarters. We wish our own car had as easy a standard shift, and that it was coupled to as slipless a clutch. You can do true speed shifts in the Dodge time after time without a sign of weariness from it. The engine which provides all this punch is essentially the same as you'll find in the all-new '55 Plymouth. It departs from recent Chrysler practice in that the combustion chambers are only partially hemispherical. Valves are offset for better breathing and have hydraulic tappets." His concluding remark was, "Our Dodge was hotter than a Hamtramck sausage."

Proving the Power of the New Light-Duty V-8 Engine

Dodge Truck engineers knew they had the world's highest horsepower engine for low-tonnage pickups, panels, and stakes. But they wanted some way to introduce this 145hp Power-Dome V-8 engine to the public before making it available for sale. Here's how Dodge Truck officials proved the power of their new engine:

1. *50,000-Mile Endurance Run:* A Dodge half-ton pickup was driven 50,000mi in fifty days—the equivalent of four years of regular service—without a mechanical breakdown.

Ralph M. Wescott of Largo, Florida, is the owner of this outstanding 23,000mi, 1957 D100 Sweptside pickup in original condition. It has the 230 six and an automatic transmission with push-button controls.

2. *AAA-Supervised Acceleration Test:* At Bonneville Salt Flats, Utah, under strict AAA supervision, several similar half-ton pickups equipped with Power-Dome V-8 engines accelerated from zero to 60mph in just 17 seconds. This time compared favorably with that of the best stock cars of the time.

3. *AAA-Supervised Economy Run:* Next came a 714mi Economy Run from Bonneville Salt Flats, Utah, to Pikes Peak, Colorado. And the same Dodge pickup demonstrated its sensational economy by averaging more than 22mpg. This is better than the 21.84mpg averaged by all stock cars in the 1954 Mobilgas Economy Run. The Dodge trucks crossed mountains and deserts, and went through city traffic, with every mile under AAA supervision. They carried a 500lb payload, as well as the driver and a rider. Regular gasoline was used.

4. *AAA-Supervised Pikes Peak Climb:* Finally, the truck was driven up Pikes Peak carrying a 500lb load, and again the trial was under strict AAA supervision. It reached the 14,110ft summit of Pikes Peak in 20 minutes, 46.8 seconds. The fastest climb ever made by an American stock car took 20 minutes, 28.4 seconds.

Other Mechanical Improvements

A host of improvement to make Dodge pickups more dependable, safer, easier to operate, and more economical were introduced. We will briefly cover only the more important upgrades.

Transmissions: A new three-speed transmission with higher speed ratios was introduced as the standard for half-ton six-cylinder models. The former heavy-duty three-speed transmission was made the standard for half-ton eight-cylinder models and for all three-quarter- and one-ton models.

The Truck-O-Matic was continued for half- and three-quarter-ton trucks.

This California black and white beauty has V-8 power.

The Famous Sweptside D100, 1957-1959

The story of the marvelous Dodge Sweptside could not be told without also describing Dodge Truck's Special Equipment Group (SEG). The SEG worked mainly with fleet buyers requesting special or modified equipment to meet their needs, but also worked with buyers interested in only a single truck. The SEG was empowered to make changes to standard Dodge trucks as long as the altered truck remained safe. Because the SEG did not require a release from central engineering, it was able to quickly and efficiently solve individual customer problems.

The SEG may help explain why collectors occasionally find a Dodge truck that varies from standard in some way. If the change appears to be something done at the factory, chances are very good that you are dealing with an SEG modification. The SEG is the reason we can't say, "That is not correct; that was never offered."

In 1957, Chevrolet's Cameo Carrier was in its third year, and Ford had just released its exciting new part-car, part-pickup, the Ranchero. Ford and Chevy made Dodge look bad because Dodge had no competitive model. Ford added to Dodge's woes in 1957 by announcing a new cab-wide "Styleside" pickup. Dodge dealers pressured the factory for something to sell against the Fords and Chevys.

Joe Berr, then-manager of the SEG, knew Dodge Truck had to react quickly. His challenge was to develop a new product without spending a lot of money (which he didn't have) on tooling and engineering, and to do it fast.

He had an idea. Joe appropriated from the Dodge car assembly plant a pair of rear fenders and a rear bumper from a 1957 Dodge two-door Suburban Station Wagon. In the SEG shop he removed the stock rear fenders from a D100 116in wheelbase Custom Cab pickup and welded the station wagon fenders to the cargo box. The station wagon's rear bumper fit like a glove, but the tailgate had to be cut down to fit between the long fenders. Chrome trim pieces, custom-made to fit the cab, continued the line running forward from the station wagon fenders. He added a two-tone paint job, full chrome wheel covers, and wide white sidewalls, and he had it: one of the most exciting and interesting collector trucks of all time.

A few key Dodge truck dealers evaluated the new creation. "Build it," they all said. "We can sell this beauty!"

The 1957 Dodge truck line featured "Forward Look Styling," a phrase and styling look borrowed from Dodge cars of 1957. The Forward Look consisted of hooded headlights and forward-thrusting front fender lines. An optional Power Dome V-8 engine, which could be coupled to the industry's first push-button-controlled automatic transmission, outperformed the veteran flat-head six. The Sweptside could also be equipped with power steering and power brakes, which made it very driveable as well as a high-styled pickup.

Sweptsides were never assembled on the production line with other pickups, but rather were built outside by a custom shop. (Unfortunately, the name of that shop is unknown.) Thus, one will find differences from truck to truck. For example, if you find a Sweptside with

Everyone's favorite—the 1957 Dodge D100 Sweptside pickup. This is one of only a few official photographs of the 1957 Sweptside.

Sweptsides were not available until late in the model year.

the small back window, be assured that it was built that way to order. It may not make sense to today's truck collectors, but it did to someone.

Truck collectors prize Dodge Sweptsides as one of the most desirable, collectible light trucks of the fifties. Sweptsides are appreciated for their beauty as well as for their scarcity. Introduced in mid-year 1957, Sweptsides only had one full year of production—1958. Production ceased in early 1959 with the advent of Dodge's new Sweptline pickups.

Aft-Type Steering: Aft-type steering features the steering gear mounted ahead of the front axle, with the drag link running from the steering gear rearward to the front axle. Aft-type steering was made standard for all trucks from half-ton through two-and-a-half-ton.

Frames: V-8 Era truck frames were entirely reengineered to permit the use of either six- or eight-cylinder engines in the same frame. An extra crossmember was added to all frames except the four-ton model, where the engine acted as a crossmember. The new crossmember supporting the rear end of the engine was located ahead of the transmission, under the clutch housing, which permitted removal of the transmission without disturbing the engine.

Clutch and Brake Pedals: Both pedals and the master cylinder were unit-mounted to the frame independently of the engine, eliminating engine movement and vibration from the pedals. The pedals were also of a new two-piece design. In addition, the pedals were now covered with rubber pedal pads.

Duane Geir, owner of Fargo's Finest Auto Body Shop in Fargo, North Dakota, is the owner of this beautiful pair. On the left is an original 1955 Custom Regal V-8 with a four-speed and only 58,000mi. It has been repainted. The 1957 half-ton has a V-8 with automatic, radio, chrome front bumper, and dual exhausts. This truck was totally restored in Duane's shop. Both trucks are painted Bermuda Coral and Mojave Beige.

1954-1960

For the purposes of this book, we have labeled the trucks Dodge built from 1954 through 1960 as the V-8 Era trucks. Officially though, according to to the Dodge Truck engineering department, they were referred to as the C-Series of 1954 through 1956, the K-Series of 1957, the L-Series of 1958, the M-Series of 1959, and the P-Series of 1960.

C-Series of 1954 through 1956

The C-Series was further broken down into the C-1 Series of 1954 through mid-year 1955 and the C-3 Series of mid-year 1955 through 1956. We find, in effect, that the C-Series consisted of two sub-series of about eighteen months each. Except for very minor mechanical and appearance updates, all changes were made in mid-year 1955

A very rare truck is this 1957 D100 half-ton panel. The black rubber molding below the headlights is nonoriginal. It was installed by a former owner before Larry Haatoja of Minneapolis, Minnesota, purchased it.

The Sweptside D100 half-ton pickup was continued for 1958.

A 1958 half-ton pickup. The side-mounted spare was an extra-cost option. The standard spare tire carrier was underslung ahead of the rear bumper. This truck is equipped with the large rear window.

with the introduction of the C-3 Series. A summary here will help clear up any confusion.

C-1 Series—from fall 1953 to April 1955.
- Up to June 1954, it was powered by 218 L-6.
- After June 1954 the L-6 engine changed to the 230 L-6 and the 241 V-8 became an optional engine for the half- through one-ton.

C-3 Series—from April 1955 to introduction of K-Series in fall of 1956.
- New cab with wraparound windshield, and wraparound rear window as an extra-cost option.
- Four levels of cab trim—Standard, De Luxe, Custom, and Custom Regal
- Fully automatic Chrysler-built PowerFlite transmission for light-duty models
- Lightweight half-ton model C-3-BL6 pickup
- New 260 V-8 of 169hp

The Sweptline cargo box was new for 1959. Dodge only used this cargo box for two years and then sold its tooling to Studebaker. Studebaker mounted this box on its early sixties Champ pickups.

- Overdrive unit for half-ton pickups only
  C-3 Series—(Engineering Series 400) from May 1956 to September 1956
- New 270 V-8 of 172hp
- New two-ton 4WD model "HW"
- Twelve-volt ignition becomes standard
- Flattened flare boards
- New Town Wagon companion to the Town Panel
- "Job-Rated" fender badges replaced by "Forward Look" emblems
- New parking brake lever under left side of dash
- Low-side cargo box discontinued

C-3 Series of April 1955: New Cab

The C-Series trucks put more emphasis than ever on driver comfort and visibility. The cab was redesigned with a new wraparound windshield as standard equipment and a wraparound rear window as extra-cost equipment. Dodge marketing called this new cab a "Pilot House" cab because its "Full Circle" visibility gave a vision area of fully ninety-eight percent glass. Front and rear corner posts were as thin in section as safety allowed.

The cab interior was restyled with new colors and trim materials for driver comfort. Cabs were now available in four trim levels, from Standard to De Luxe to Custom to Custom Regal. Each was more luxurious than the last.

New Model

The one new light-duty model was the C-3-BL6, which was a light-duty pickup offered only with a six-cylinder engine. Also, no single-lever seat adjuster was provided. Instead, one had to remove four bolts, adjust the seat, and then retighten the bolts! Gross weight of this truck was only 4,250lb, compared to 5,100lb for the standard half-ton pickup. It was intended for customers who only had light loads to move and were concerned with economy.

New Transmissions

An overdrive unit, for half-ton pickups only, became available for the first time, but only with the standard three-speed transmission. The Chrysler-built PowerFlite fully automatic transmission was available for all light-duty models.

1956 C-3 Series (after May 1956)

Cabs, bodies, sheet metal, and ornamentation (except "Job-Rated" replaced with "Forward Look" badges) remained the same as in 1955 (after C-3/T-400 of May 1956). A 270 V-8 with 172hp became the standard V-8 for light-duty models. The only new model was the Town Wagon, a passenger/cargo version of the Town Panel. The only other change of note was the flattening of the flare boards on all pickups.

1957 K-Series

The basic package of the V-8 Era Trucks was put into place with the C-3 Series cab in late 1955. With yearly updates to make it even more comfortable and easier to drive, this cab served Dodge through the 1960 model year. If you are familiar with Dodge, you are aware that this same cab was also used for the C model line of medium-duty and heavy-duty low cab-forward trucks through the 1975 model year, at which time Dodge dropped out of the heavy-duty truck business.

While cabs and bodies remained the same, the styling of front-end sheet metal changed from year to year, reflecting engineering refinements as well as improvements to appearance. This year was an excellent example of a change in front-end sheet metal styling to bring about not only a style change but also an engineering change that made these trucks easier to service.

Overall, 1957's styling theme was picked up from Chrysler's automobile styling direction touted as the "Forward Look." The idea was to make the truck appear as if it was moving even while standing still. The engineering advancement was the change to a one-piece, alligator-style hood. Dodge engineers designed the new hood to open upright at 90 degrees for major work, or to 48 degrees for routine servicing.

Engineering Improvements

Two major driveline engineering improvements for light-duty models were the addition of the three-speed push-button automatic transmission coupled to a larger, more powerful 315 V-8 engine. The push-button control selector was mounted at the left side of the dashboard. The driver selected his drive range, pushed the button, and then stepped on the accelerator. It was a truly modern engineering feature. The V-8's horsepower rating rose from 172hp to 204hp (with an increase of 45ci)—a whopping 32 percent increase! The six-cylinder engine's rating increased from 115hp to 120hp through an increase in its compression ratio.

New Parking Brake

Because the push-button transmission was not equipped with a parking position, an improved parking brake was required. Starting with the C-3/T400 Series, Dodge engineers answered with an adjustable hand-brake lever located to the driver's left. This brake was of the lever-action-type, which was fast and easy to set and release, without squeezing or turning. A quick turn of the knurled knob on the end of the hand lever took up cable

Edward Ivener of Scottsdale, Arizona, owns this original-condition, blue and white, 1959 Dodge Sweptside D100 pickup. It has a 318 V-8 with automatic, power steering, and big back window.

slack, and the brake was back into perfect adjustment. A disadvantage with the new brake was that it was easy to bump with the knees while getting in and out, which caused the handle to fall, disengaging the brake!

New Tires

All light-duty models were equipped with tubeless tires. Advantages were lower weight, cooler running, quicker and easier servicing, and added durability. Tube-type tires were still available, however, at no extra-cost.

Cab Features

Only two basic cabs were offered this year— Standard and Custom— compared to four in 1956. The only real difference was in their trim levels and available standard equipment. Interior colors and seat design changed, as did the style of door handles, latches, and locks.

Expanded 4WD Models

After eleven years of building the only one-ton, factory-built 4WD pickup in the industry, Dodge management chose to expand upon this important market segment by adding half- and three-quarter-ton conventional cab 4WD pickups. In 1956 Dodge rolled out the W500, a two-ton 4WD conventional cab Power Wagon. Dodge now offered the W100 on 108in and 116in wheelbases, the W200 on a 116in wheelbase, the original W300 one-ton military type on a 126in wheelbase, and the W500 on 156in and 174in wheelbases. One year later, the W300 conventional cab made its debut. At that time the model designation of the original Power Wagon changed to WM300 (M for military type styling). All 4WDs of this era were badged as Power Wagons.

However, the new conventional cab 4WDs were not the same as the original Power Wagon. These new entries were built using outside-manufactured components, not the Chrysler-engineered and -built components of the original. Nevertheless, these are tough trucks and are interesting collector finds. Unfortunately, most of these early ones were worked to death, and consequently, not many are available. The few remaining ones are highly prized by collectors.

1958 L-Series
This was another year of modest refinements and improvements in both styling and mechanical features while continuing with the basic cab from mid-1955.

New Front-End Sheet Metal
Changes in front-end styling dramatically enhanced Dodge's already good looks due to a new wider, lower hood, all-new grille, and a heavy-duty wraparound front bumper. The smart new grille consisted of four horizontal bars and dual, wide-spaced headlights. The dual headlights added to the truck's heavier, huskier appearance, but also aided night driving safety.

The primary reason for the redesign was to obtain an engine compartment as wide as possible to allow for maximum service accessibility. This was accomplished by a complete new design of front fender housings, the addition of engine compartment splash shields, and the use of a new full-width hood. With the extra space now available under the wide hood, the battery was moved from below the driver's floor to inside the engine compartment for easier servicing.

Don Lawrence of Fargo, North Dakota, owns two Sweptside D100 pickups. The truck on the left is a 1957, and the black beauty on the right is a 1959. Both trucks have small rear windows and standard cabs. Yes, Dodge did build Sweptsides with these low-line features.

Cab Interior
The cab interior was restyled with new trim and new color combinations in upholstery selections. In keeping with its safety theme for 1958, Dodge engineers changed to a deep center steering wheel, added built-in turn signals, and painted the hand-brake lever Dodge Truck Red. For the first time Dodge offered as an option a ceiling-mounted transistorized radio, located between the sun visors for easy tuning and far removed from engine noise.

New Model
Dodge's growing family of 4WD models was again expanded in 1958 with the roll-out of the W300 with either six or V-8 power. Features included 10,000lb maximum GVW, Spicer front and rear axles, the same transfer case and power take-off as the W100 and W200 models for maximum interchangeability, heavy-duty frame, and standard four-speed transmission, with the three-speed LoadFlite automatic as an option.

1959 M-Series
While in reality the 1959 M-Series trucks were another model of the V-8 Era, so many changes and improvements were made that it leads one to think these were all-new trucks. These new trucks were so handsome they gave the impression that they also offered passenger car ride and handling. Beauty they had, but it was a working beauty, for these smart new trucks offered more cargo space and payload than their competitors.

New Front Styling
Front styling change amounted only to a new grille insert with an expanded metal design featuring eight rectangular openings. However, this simple change totally altered the front end appearance. The new, cleaner, more sophisticated look was much more pleasing to the eye. The new grille was topped off by an updated Dodge nameplate on the front of the hood. New ornamentation on the hood sides and fender sides completed the new front styling.

Cab Changes
Cab changes included new concealed running boards on light-duty trucks for both style and easier entry. New upholstery fabrics and color choices for both Standard and Custom Cab interiors were offered, as well as door trim panels and roof headlining.

A completely new instrument panel brought new utility and beauty, and prevented instrument reflection on the windshield at night. A new hooded instrument panel located all gauges in a tight cluster directly in front of the driver for fast and accurate checking. The glove box was relocated to a conventional location at the driver's right.

Engineering Improvements

A new hydraulically operated clutch made driving and shifting smoother and easier. The master cylinder for the clutch was mounted on the firewall for easy service access. Both the brake and clutch pedals were suspended for new convenience and driver comfort, and to eliminate drafts from the floor.

Also new was a 318 V-8 engine with integral oil filter. This new V-8 featured 8.25:1 compression ratio and 205hp.

A new 3.54:1 rear axle ratio for the D100 provided better top speed and maximum fuel economy.

New Model: The Famous Sweptline

As if all of the above were not enough, Dodge designers added the smartest-looking pickup on the highway in the new Sweptline. The sleek, smooth-sided, new Sweptline was not only handsome, but practical, too. Loads of space in this new, wider pickup box translated into bigger payloads. Hardwood floors continued for the narrower cargo boxes, but a sleek metal floor was standard for Sweptline pickups. Dodge marketing designated the original-type pickup cargo box the Utility body, which was later changed to Utiline to differentiate it from the modern Sweptline. The glamorous Sweptside's career ended in January 1959 when marketing pulled its plug.

1960 P-Series

In 1960 Dodge Truck took its biggest stride forward in a third of a century. That big stride was limited to medium-duty and heavy-weight trucks, however, which are outside of the scope of this book. This was the year Dodge rolled out its LCF (low-cab-forward) models, which became the mainstay of the medium- and heavy-tonnage offerings until Dodge dropped out of those market segments in 1975.

Appearance Changes

A new grille insert of extruded aluminum provided a distinctive touch of long-lasting beauty. Another new touch was painting the Dodge nameplate, located just above the new grille, black with chrome letters; in 1959 the letters in the Dodge name had been painted red with a chrome background. New ornamentation on the hood sides and a slight change in the chrome trim pieces on the doors completed the appearance changes for 1960.

A 1960 D100 half-ton Utiline pickup. This was the last year of the V-8 Era trucks.

Custom Cab Equipment

Available as custom cab equipment were an armrest for driver's side; variable-speed electric wipers; insulated dash lining; sound-absorbent door panels; insulated hardboard headlining; Saran seat upholstery with vinyl facings and bolsters; foam rubber seat and seat back padding; and dual sun visors.

V-8 Era Truck Engines						
Half-Ton and Three-Quarter-Ton Trucks						
Year	Cyl	Bore x Stroke	CID	BHP	Torque	Compression
1954	6	3.25 x 4.375	218	100 @ 3600	177lb/ft	7.1:1
1954	6	3.25 x 4.625	230.2	110 @ 3600	194lb/ft	7.25:1
One-Ton Trucks						
1954	6	3.25 x 4.625	230.2	110 @ 3600	194lb/ft	7.25:
Optional V-8 Engine, Late Production Only: All Models						
1954	8	3.4375 x 3.25	241.4	145 @ 4400	215lb/ft	7.5:1
Note: From this time on both engines are used in all light trucks, with the six-cylinder standard and the V-8 optional.						
1955	6	3.25 x 4.625	230.2	110 @ 3600	194lb/ft	7.25:1
1955	8	3.563 x 3.25	259.2	169 @ 4400	243lb/ft	7.6:1
Early						
1956	6	3.25 x 4.625	230.2	115 @ 3600	201lb/ft	7.6:1
1956	8	3.563 x 3.25	259.2	169 @ 4400	243lb/ft	7.6:1
Late						
1956	8	3.63 x 3.259	269.6	172 @ 4400	262lb/ft	8.0:1
1957-						
1958	6	3.25 x 4.625	230.2	120 @ 3600	202lb/ft	7.9:1
1957-						
1958	8	3.63 x 3.80	314.61	204 @ 4400	290lb/ft	8.1:1
1959-						
1960	6	3.25 x 4.625	230.2	120 @ 3600	202lb/ft	7.9:1
1959-						
1960	8	3.91 x 3.312	318.14	200 @ 3600	286lb/ft	8.25:1

Chapter 7

Sweptline Era Trucks 1961-1971

★★	1961-1971 Half-ton pickup
★★★	1961-1971 Half-ton 4WD pickup
★★★	1961-1971 Half-ton Town Panel and Town Wagon
★★★★	1961-1971 Half-ton 4WD Town Panel and Town Wagon
★★★★★	1964-1967 Half-ton Custom Sports Special
★★	1961-1971 Three-quarter- and one-ton 4WD pickups
★★	1961-1971 Three-quarter- and one-ton 4WD stake and platform
★★★★	1968-1971 Half-ton Adventurer pickups
★★★★	1961-1968 One-ton military-style Power Wagon pickups
★★★	1961-1968 One-ton military-style Power Wagons with special bodies

The decade of the fifties was somewhat of a roller coaster at Dodge Truck. Sales in the first three years were excellent. In the fourth year, 1953, sales dropped alarmingly. The three mid-years, 1954-1956, were flat, with a low sales rate not experienced since the thirties. The last three years fell to a disasterous level with 1958, a recession year for the nation's economy, dropping to the sickening total of only 64,948 trucks of all sizes. Sales in 1960 continued at this same low level. However, 1960 was the last year for the by-this-time veteran V-8 Era trucks.

A load of 1961 Dodge pickups on their way to dealers. The half-ton sitting above the tractor was a basic pickup. Note how the very light-scale 1961 grille seems to almost disappear. That was the reason why the grille was restyled in 1962.

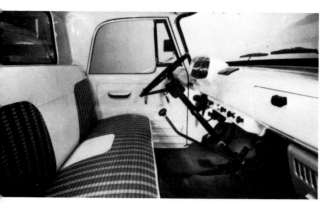

The cab interior of a 1961 deluxe cab pickup.

The interior of a 1961 Sweptline pickup's cargo box. This cargo box was used until mid-year 1965.

Dodge Truck found itself in 1960 in the same position it had been in 1932. That is, it had low sales, an outdated design, an obsolete engine (the L-6), and a rather bleak outlook. As you might conclude, Dodge had been working on all-new light- and medium-duty trucks for several years; these were targeted to debut in the fall of 1960 as the 1961 models. If we count the Commercial Cars built by the original Dodge Brothers Company as the first generation of Dodge trucks, and the all-new Chryslerized trucks of 1933-1960 as the second generation of Dodge Trucks, then the Sweptline Era trucks introduced for 1961 were then the third generation of Dodge trucks.

The 1961 Sweptline Era trucks were about as close as a new model can come to being entirely new. Certainly they looked the part with all-new cab and cargo box sheet metal featuring a longer, lower, and wider modern style. And surprise of surprises, Dodge marketing named the new half-ton pickup *Dart*. This was the first Dodge truck to be named in the same manner as car lines were. Up until this time, all names for trucks had been descriptive: Power Wagon, Route Van, Town Panel, Town Wagon, etc. The name *Dart* was borrowed, of course, from Dodge's very successful Dart intermediate-size car line.

Frames

Underneath the new sheet metal was a new drop-center frame for half- and three-quarter-ton models. The purpose of the drop-center frame was to set the cab 3in lower, easing entry and exit through wider door openings. Like their heavier-duty cousins, one-ton trucks were built on straight frames with heavier, deeper side rails. All frames were longer, which produced wheelbase lengths of 114in, 122in, and 133in for half-, three-quarter-, and one-ton models, respectively.

Engines

The standard 318 V-8 engine was carried over without change. All new, on the other hand, was the slant-six, available in two sizes. The 170 was reserved for the lightest-duty half-tons only, with the 225 installed in all other light-duties except the conventional cab Power Wagons and the original military-style Power Wagon. The time-proven 251 L-6 powered both of these trucks plus the medium-duty W500 Power Wagon.

Models

No new models swept in with the new Sweptline Era trucks except for the addition of a three-quarter-ton forward-control model. But on the other hand, none were dropped either.

An interesting anomaly with the Sweptline models occurred with the Town Wagon and Town Panel. These two popular trucks in either 2WD or 4WD configurations dated back to the mid-fifties and were built on a 108in wheelbase. Changing the standard half-ton's wheelbase to 114in created an interesting situation, because the Town Wagon and Town Panel did not share the same sheet metal as the pickups. To accommodate the longer wheelbase for 1961, the front wheel well opening was moved forward, which compromised the original design and created a slightly ungainly look. The casual observer, however, might never notice.

Alternator

All light-duty models featured the new alternator. It replaced the conventional generator—an industry first and, in a short time, an industry standard. The alternator charged even at slow engine speeds; it was smaller and lighter than a generator; and it promoted longer battery life.

The interior of a 1961 Utiline pickup's cargo box. This cargo box stayed in production until 1985.

Cab Choices

For 1961, cab choices were simple—either spartan or high style. For those who wanted a basic, hard-working, no-frills truck, the standard cab was available. Or, if a buyer wanted the top-of-the-line, he could opt for the custom cab.

1962-1964

The soft point in the 1961 Sweptline Era's styling was its grille. It most aptly could be described as weak. It was too light in scale—so much so that it almost appeared to be nonexistent—and looked particularly bad on medium-duty models. It just wouldn't do to have a truck that looked weak!

So Dodge designers changed to a new grille in 1962. It's truly remarkable what a big improvement can be wrought from such a simple change. The new grille was in itself a study in simplicity. But it accomplished what Dodge designers set out to do—that is, give the front of the truck a more masculine look. The model number plate was attached to the front center of the grille. When used with the standard cab, the grille was painted Sand Dune White; for use with the custom cab, it was chrome-plated. The only other appearance change was placing a Dodge nameplate on each front fender.

Other Changes and Improvements

We don't expect many changes in the second year of an all-new truck line, and that is exactly what happened. The only changes of note affecting pickups, other than the new grille, included making complete chassis and body undercoating a factory-applied, extra-cost option. The inside-of-box spare tire carrier, which was standard with Utiline pickups, was replaced by a new, underslung-type carrier; lock-out front wheel hubs became available as extra-cost equipment for all light-duty 4WD models, including the original Power Wagon. And the hydraulic stop light switch was replaced by a mechanical switch.

1963

In the third year of the Sweptline Era, no changes were made in styling, ornamentation, or paint colors. Instead, Dodge engineers concentrated on those items that would improve durability, economy, and performance. In fact, for 1963, Dodge management announced it would discontinue the practice of presenting new models during the industry's usual new model introduction season.

New Engine

After thirty years, the last flathead six disappeared from Dodge light-duty trucks (except for the original Power Wagon), when a new version of the slant-six engine was installed in one-ton conventional cab Power Wagons. Its replacement was

A 1961 Dodge one-ton chassis cab. This was the last era in which one-ton models were built on a chassis with straight frame rails. Although not shown on this truck, outside running boards were standard equipment for one-tonners.

Crew cab three-quarter-ton pickups like this 1962 model are of interest to many collectors, who admire their usefulness.

Chrysler's Slant-Six Engine

By Carl Friberg

Here is one of the most indestructible, durable, and reliable engines ever made. Introduced for the 1960 model year, the slant-six was developed in the late fifties as a replacement for the smaller L-6s in light-duty Dodge trucks and MoPar cars, as well as for larger-block sixes used in bigger US- and Canadian-built MoPar cars and trucks. It was a far superior design.

The slant-six's introduction coincided with the new compact Valiant. These cars used the 170 version, which had a 1in lower block than the 225 engine used in regular-size Plymouths and Dodges that year. Engine displacement and serial numbers were stamped on a machined pad on the upper right side of the block near the coil. Earlier engines had letters for the year and first and second digits of the displacement, while later ones had only the full three-number displacement size.

For 1961, smaller Dodge trucks also received the new slant-six (usually the 225 version). Since car hoods were lower during the sixties than in earlier years, the engine was inclined 30 degrees to the right.

(*Author's note:* It is a commonly held belief that the reason Chrysler's first modern OHV six was "slanted" was to reduce the engine's overall height. The lower engine height supposedly enabled designers to lower the car's hood for appearance. This is only partially true. Slanting the engine's block did indeed result in lowering the engine's overall height, but that was a side benefit, not the principal reason.

The engineers set out to reduce the engine's length. The Valiant's design team wanted the engine shorter to leave them with more interior space. By rolling the engine over, they could provide plenty of room to place the water pump on the engine's side. The lower height was a surprise benefit. So were the long manifold runners, and the new position of the carburetor and air cleaner off to the side.

A lower hood height has been a major consideration only in the last few years, since designers have been forced to lower drag coefficients for fuel economy. —DB)

This "slant" also enabled the use of a gently curved intake manifold for a more equal distribution of fuel/air mixture to all cylinders and less restriction of intake flow. Valves canted into the wedge-shaped combustion chambers were also used for the same reason.

The 225 was undersquare (longer stroke than bore) and was one of the last new engines with this once-common design. (This was also the last inline six for Chrysler Corporation.) The engine's slanted posture made the longer stroke possible as well as the use of individual intake and exhaust tubing.

The intake and exhaust valves alternated, with no exhaust valves adjacent to each other, so there were no localized hot spots. Valves were actuated by rocker arms of the shaft pivot design introduced in 1955 by Chevrolet on its "mouse motor" V-8.

Other distinguishing features were the separate distributor and oil pump drives, both mounted on the right side of the block about mid-point, with the distributor above the externally mounted oil pump. The distributor was driven from above the camshaft, while the oil pump was driven underneath the same cam gear. This was unlike the usual layout, in which the distributor and oil pump were on opposite sides of the block. The oil filter and oil pump used the same integral housing; it was fastened at the rear of the oil pump housing, thus eliminating the earlier engine's external oil line. Around 1965, Dodge switched from canister-type filters to spin-on filters for light-duty trucks; canisters were still usually used on medium-duty trucks.

The spark plugs, completely sealed by rubber boots, were recessed into the head, on the right side inside deep tubes. The intake and exhaust manifolds were on the engine's left side, as was the starter. The fuel pump was on the right side, near the front. The forged crankshaft turned on four main bearings, and camshaft drive was by a chain.

To save weight, several add-on components were made of aluminum. 1961 was the first year for the alternator in the US, where Chrysler Corporation led the industry. In Canada, alternators were optional equipment in 1961 but became standard in 1963. In 1966, the intake manifold was changed to cast iron, and the alternator moved to the engine's left side.

Over the years, slant-sixes used one bore size—3.40in—but three stroke lengths: 3.125in for the 170, 3.64in for the 198 (available from 1970-1974), and 4.12in on the 225. In 1970, the 198 engine, which used the 225 block with shorter connecting rods, replaced the 170.

Around 1963, a PCV system replaced the road draft crankcase ventilation. Also in 1963, a new premium 225 was introduced for medium-duty trucks. The first of these engines were painted red, and the later ones were yellow. They featured a roller timing chain, stellite-faced exhaust valve seat inserts, bimetal connecting rod bearings, roto caps on exhaust valves, a shot-peened crankshaft, a high-volume oil pump (recognizable by a larger housing), a higher-lift camshaft, and shorter, stiffer valve springs.

In 1968, the number of freeze plugs changed from three to five; earlier three-plug engines had the two freeze or core plugs lower on the block with the center plug up higher. Five-plug engines were set up with the core plugs in a row, positioned in the higher location. Also in 1968, the crankshaft end hub increased in size from 1.5in to 1.75in.

To meet emission control standards, camshaft duration was changed in 1971 from 232 degrees to 244 degrees. This was done to compensate for combustion chamber and carburetor modifications. Around 1972, the engine color was changed to blue, and electronic ignition became optional. In 1974, the 198 engine was dropped. A significant change, to cut construction costs, was an inferior cast crankshaft that was substituted for the forged crank. A "Super Six" with a Carter BBD carburetor and aluminum two-barrel manifold was offered in 1977.

Two types of starters were used through the years, one with a direct armature-to-starter drive gear and another with double reduction gearing. The latter had a larger diameter housing. For 1962, engines were equipped with starters having built-in solenoids. At least some trucks used the earlier separate solenoid-type starters through about 1964.

This is the best engine Chrysler ever made. It has proven to be dependable and durable, and many have faithfully logged 100,000 miles and more. Two aluminum versions were made, one with cast-iron cylinder sleeves, the other with an all-aluminum block. These engines were available into 1962, then discontinued. A slant-six diesel was developed but not produced.

Chrysler Corporation discontinued the slant-six in cars in 1983, and about that time slant-six production moved from the US to Mexico, where labor costs were lower. This engine was last available in trucks in 1986, although industrial versions are still being made.

the premium version of the 225 slant-six called the 225-2. The premium 225-2 was also used in all ton-and-a-half and two-ton medium-duty trucks. Premium features included a roller timing chain, bimetal connecting rod bearings, stellite-faced exhaust valves, roto-caps on exhaust valves, and polyacrylic valve stem seals. Gross torque at 215lb-ft and horsepower at 140 were the same as for the nonpremium 225-1.

1964

In line with the new policy of continuing year-long introduction of improvements, no changes were announced for Dodge light-duty models for 1964. Dodge engineers and management had their plates full with an all-new line of compact trucks, while at the same time preparing a line of diesel-powered tandem-tilt-cab trucks for market. One new model joined the pickup lineup, and that was the Custom Sports Special (see sidebar).

1965

Maintaining the policy of not bringing out a "new" truck in the fall (in contrast to the industry's usual practice), the old model carried over for 1965 without change. This year wasn't to be one without change, however, for in the spring of 1965 Dodge unleashed a dramatically improved truck on the buying public.

Second Series 1965

These trucks are of special interest to the collector because they were the first new trucks from Dodge in quite some time in which we see a real effort being made to make the trucks more comfortable and attractive. The big explosion in pickup sales hadn't quite arrived yet in 1965, but the signs that pickup sales would take off with jet speed in the near future were apparent to perceptive observers. Dodge management read the signs and positioned themselves to take advantage of the coming strong pickup market.

New Styling, Appearance, and Comfort

Dodge pickups were sharper and more distinguished looking in 1965, with an all-new grille and headlight treatment. While not a major styling uplift, the new grille did deliver a more distinctive appearance. Along with the new grille, a new Appearance Package was also offered. It consisted of a chrome grille, bright mylar molding around the windshield and rear window, bright drip moldings, custom nameplates, Dodge Delta ornament on the "B" posts, bright trim on the instrument panel's hood and around knobs and dials, bright molding on the instrument panel, textured metal trim on door panels, white steering wheel, and chrome horn ring (on half- and three-quarter-ton models only).

And for Sweptline pickups only, full-length side moldings were available. These were painted white for dark-colored trucks or black for light-colored trucks. A new Comfort Package included a left armrest, right sun visor, cigar lighter, full-foam

The restyled grille on this 1962 half-ton Sweptline pickup is much improved over 1961. This basic design stayed as is, without change, until mid-year 1965.

The Custom Sports Special's black vinyl bucket seats can be seen through the windshield of this 1964 model. This truck could have been ordered with a slant-six, 318, 426, or 426 Hemi!

seat back with new custom trim in three color choices, and additional insulation.

Engineering and Pickup Cargo Box Improvements

For starters, the wheelbases for half- and three-quarter-ton pickups were increased to 128in, which improved weight distribution, especially for pickup camper users. The Sweptline's tailgate opening was increased to 65in to make loading and unloading easier. A new, one-hand tailgate latch for Sweptlines saved time and improved appearance. The cargo box on Sweptline pickups had flat-on-the-top wheel wells to save space and to aid in loading cargo. The box was now full height, with double-wall construction for better strength and appearance. The long box was increased from 7.5ft to 8ft in length—the industry standard to this day.

Prices Remained the Same

In order to demonstrate their desire to become a bigger force in the pickup sales race, Dodge gave potential buyers all of the above improvements plus no change in prices!

Summary

With new styling, plus appearance, comfort, and convenience packages, the second series 1965 Dodge pickups were much improved over the earlier years of this era and are more desirable today. Select a model with as many optional equipment items as possible. Prices for these models are very attractive.

1966

The second series 1965 models were released so late in the model year that they could even be

considered 1966 models. Thus, the 1966 trucks were identical to those of the second series of 1965.

1967-1968

Knowing Dodge as we do, we didn't expect a "new" truck in the fall of 1966. We expected one just a little later in the year, right? Right. And Dodge management did not let us down. They gave us a restyled model as a 1967-and-a-half truck.

When W. Fowler of Ringling, Oklahoma, found this 1964 Custom Sports Special in California, he didn't know what he had. He assumed its black stripes were something the original owner added, and he removed them. When he later realized he had a very special truck, he immediately began to restore it. This Custom Sports Special has the slant-six, automatic, and only 70,000mi.

Custom Sports Special 1964-1967

One has to admire the forward-thinking Dodge Truck management that introduced the first Custom Sports Special in 1964. They hit the market dead on the head, with a bases-loaded home run. If we look at what was happening in the world of truck sales, we notice that Dodge caught the public's voracious appetite for pickups just as it was taking off like a space shuttle off its launch pad. In 1964, truck sales reached the levels of the early fifties, but as time has shown, the curve climbed steeply year after year.

Dodge Truck management considered the entire market and concluded that truck buyers wanted the following from their pickups: A rugged, powerful, heavy-duty truck for hauling or pulling campers. A plush, comfortable cab interior with amenities for two demanding travelers. Tasteful styling to fit into any neighborhood, country club, or work site. Power and performance to suit the most demanding motoring enthusiast.

After almost thirty years of high-style and high-performance pickups, we do not fully appreciate today the contribution the Custom Sports Special made in pickup history. This is because the Custom Sports Special is almost unknown to pickup collectors. When was the last time you saw one at a truck show? Two years ago when I first wrote about them in our book *Dodge Pickups History and Restoration Guide 1918-1971,* I knew of only one. It has since been destroyed by its owner, who didn't

This 1965 Custom Sports Special owned by Greg Tomberlin is one of the rarest of the rare Dodge pickups. It is a 426 Hemi-equipped Custom Sports Special. This truck was one of two specials built for a car show or for some other promotion. Its paint and interior are nonstandard, but original.

appreciate what he had; he turned it into a street rod. Since then, four more have surfaced around the country, and at least two were originally powered by 426 Hemis! Certainly there are more, and they will be seen eventually. Custom Sports Specials were to the sixties what Sweptsides were to the fifties. These are the most collectible of all the pickups Dodge ever built.

A Custom Sports Special was not a separate model; rather, it was an Additional Factory Installed Equipment package available on all D100 and D200 chassis cab, Utiline, and Sweptline pickups. In 1965 this package sold for an extra $255.30 and consisted of the following items: two bucket seats; custom carpeting; 1in tape stripes; bright mylar molding around windshield and rear window; Dodge Delta emblems on "B" posts; bright moldings on instrument panel; bright horn ring; arm rests on both right and left sides; dual sun visors; additional insulation; console with lighter and map light; black carpet over the gas tank cover; bright radiator grille; bright drip moldings; Custom nameplates; bright trim on instrument cluster and around dials and knobs; white steering wheel; and chrome front bumper.

A second package priced at $1,235.60 called the "High-Performance Package" was also available for all D100 and D200 chassis cab, Utiline, and Sweptline pickup models. It was limited to 128in wheelbase models only. (The price list does not say the High-Performance Package had to be purchased in conjunction with the package described above.) The High-Performance Package included: 426 wedge engine; rear axle struts; rear axle ratios of 3.23, 3.55, 3.91, 3.54, or 4.1; rear spring capacity per spring of 1,750lb for D100 and 2,600lb for D200; A727 LoadFlite transmission; 8in-diameter vacuum brake booster; heavy-duty instrument cluster; power steering; and tachometer. The 426 engine air cleaner and rocker covers were chrome.

The base engine was the 225 slant-six; the 318 V-8 was optional. A three-speed transmission with column-mounted lever was standard.

In 1963, Dodge management prepared one or more preproduction test models and let automotive journalists test them. The test trucks were not yet called Custom Sports Specials, but they were very close to the actual model released one year later. The only changes were that the chrome side rails along the flare boards were dropped, as were the the carlike, full chrome wheelcovers; and the high-performance engine was the 426 instead of the 413 that had been announced originally.

Engineering Changes

At Dodge Truck, engineering concerns always take precedence over mere appearance changes. The major engineering improvement for this year was a new, larger V-8: the 383. By this time, truck manufacturers were enjoying a boom in sales of pickup campers and pickups needed to pull camping trailers of all types and sizes. So Dodge sorely needed an engine with more hauling and pulling power to fill this niche. The 383 was the first engine ever put into a Dodge truck that engineering did not modify for severe service. This occurred for two reasons. First, Dodge needed a larger engine and needed it immediately because of the tremendous pressure dealers were putting on management for a more powerful pickup. The 383 was available, since it was a standard engine option for all Chrysler-built cars. Dodge Truck engineers determined that the 383's horsepower and torque output were sizeable enough not to need premium components to stand up to truck duty.

The other engineering advancement was a new four-speed manual transmission. It featured farther-spaced second and third gears, which enabled the driver to shift down at higher speeds without overrevving the engine. Therefore, a heavily loaded camper could shift down into third on a hill and still maintain its normal highway speed.

Appearance Changes

The new model year brought a new grille and a new cab roof. The new grille featured more chrome than at anytime during the Sweptline Era. This new look was fresh and interesting. Many collectors find it more appealing than that of the previous years.

Don Lawrence's Custom Sports Special's cab interior clearly shows the original condition of its upholstery. The carpet is black, which is correct. Note the deluxe white steering wheel.

Don Lawrence of Fargo, North Dakota, is the owner of this second series 1965 Custom Sports Special with a 318, three-speed transmission, and small back window, which is rare for a high-line pickup. Don's Custom Sports Special has 90,000 original miles. Its interior and paint are also original.

This 1964 Custom Sports Special belongs to Steve Earl of Portland, Oregon. It is a rare, 426-powered truck. This truck is slated for a full restoration. As of this time, four Custom Sports Specials are known to exist. Undoubtedly, more will come to light in the future.

This was to be the last year of the Custom Sports Special. But Dodge management dropped in a new model to bridge the gap between the Custom Sports Special and the exciting up-market Adventurer pickups that rolled out one year later.

Vinyl Top Special

The new model was called the Vinyl Top Special. The black "vinyl" top was actually a specially applied paint, stippled to create a grain effect. One had to actually touch it to prove it was paint, not vinyl. Other features of the Vinyl Top Special included a chrome-bordered paint stripe along the cab and cargo box sides, twin chrome sideview mirrors, choice of five paint colors, bucket seats, center console, firewall-to-back-window deep pile carpeting, white walls, chrome bumpers, and chrome full wheel covers or mag wheel covers. This truck is of special interest to collectors due to its scarcity.

The 1968-1971 Dodge Adventurer

Dodge Truck first became interested in luxury, fashion, comfort, and convenience in 1953, when the division decided to try to attract women drivers. It promoted the half-ton pickup as a dual-purpose vehicle suited for both work and for family transportation. Dodge offered a semi-automatic transmission, tinted windows, and an upgraded interior that year. This truck was crude compared to today's trucks, yet the movement toward a more civilized truck had begun.

Dodge's Custom Sports Special, which immediately preceeded the Adventurer, was the first serious step toward marketing the pickup as an upgraded, dual-purpose vehicle. The Custom Sports Special emphasized "sports" more than duality, and thus fell short in terms of creating a true, dual-purpose truck.

The Custom Sports Special served its purpose, however, by putting in place much of what later became the norm for a high-styled luxury truck.

The Adventurer was not a specific model, but rather a "package." It really included two packages—an interior and an exterior package that came as a set, and *only* as a set.

A Dodge Truck document dated June 1967 indicates that Adventurer packages would be available for the A100 pickup, but this never happened. Dodge Truck marketing knew the A100's days were numbered and decided against it. Adventurer packages were offered only on D100 Sweptline 114in and 128in wheelbase pickups, and on D200 Sweptline 128in wheelbase pickups (both 2WD and 4WD models). It was not available on Crew Cab models. It's easy to understand the aesthetic reasons for offering the Adventurer package on Sweptline pickups but not on Utiline pickups. But I can see another reason: Dodge, as well as Ford and Chevrolet, did not want to build a narrow, fender-side-type pickup cargo box; its wooden floor and bolted-together construction were too labor-intensive and costly to build. The all-steel Sweptline cargo box was automatically welded into a single unit at less cost. It was in the best interest of all pickup manufacturers to woo customers away from the old-fashioned, narrow box. Dodge was the first builder to discontinue its narrow cargo box, in 1985, and the others have followed suit.

Because an Adventurer was a package, Dodge marketing found it easy to add, subtract, or modify to suit market conditions for promotions and the like. For example, in 1969 the Adventurer package was expanded, both interior and exterior, to create an even more high-fashion and elegant statement.

The ultimate Adventurer was new for 1970. As we have often seen in the past, truck development was an evolutionary—not revolutionary—process. So it was with the Adventurer. By 1970, Dodge designers put it all together. For 1971, the Sweptline Era's last year, three Adventurers were offered: the base Adventurer, the mid-level Adventurer Sport, and the top-of-the-line Adventurer S.E. The main difference between the Sport and the S.E. was that the S.E. had a woodgrain applique on its tailgate and lower body sides. In my opinion, the S.E. was overdone because of the woodgrain application; it might be acceptable on a station wagon, but never on a pickup.

Collectors are becoming seriously interested in 1968-1971 Adventurers, and cherish them because of what they are: beautiful, well-built trucks equipped with all the goodies. When equipped with V-8s, automatics, and full-power assists, they are very driveable. My favorites are the 1970 and the 1971 Sport models. You should look first for either one of these with V-8 and automatic and as much optional equipment as possible. Your second choice should be the 1968 and 1969 models, with the 1969 the better of the two. All Adventurers will increase in value, and, in the mean time, they will deliver a truckful of fun and enjoyment.

Dodge pickups were restyled in mid-year 1965. A half-ton 1965 D100 Sweptline is shown.

1969

The rapidly expanding personal-use factor of pickups during the sixties has resulted in a major boon for pickup collectors because most collectors prefer high-line models. The snappier a truck's looks, the more comfort and convenience options it offers, the more desirable its power train (V-8 engines, automatic transmissions), the more interest it has for most truck collectors. These pickups have the power and carrying ability of a truck, but the sporty look, ride, and driveability of a passenger car.

New Instrument Panel

For 1969, Dodge Truck engineering moved forward with giant steps in building more double-life, carlike pickups. The most important appearance change for 1969 was a redesigned, luxurious instrument panel. Protective padding ran the full length of the panel. A new cluster faceplate with edge lighting, safety controls and knobs, passenger car slide-type heater controls, and a flip-up glove compartment door completed the new tailored look. Another new standard was an energy-absorbing, 17in deep-dish steering wheel.

Tad Faubian of Portland, Oregon, owns this second series 1965 D100 half-ton pickup powered by a slant-six.

A husband takes his wife out for dinner in his high-style 1967 D100 Sweptline pickup. His Dodge is right at home mixing with society.

The US Army purchased many of these 1970 three-quarter-ton stake trucks.

The only major exterior styling change (and a welcome one, to be sure) was a redesigned hood. At long last the nonfunctional hood louvers were history.

Mechanical Improvements

The most significant engineering advancement was a ride-and-drive improvement for half- and three-quarter-ton trucks. Dodge called it "Cushioned Beam Suspension." Cushioned beam provided a smoother, more comfortable ride. Basically what engineering did was modify the old reliable I-beam-type, front-axle suspension system by adding a sway bar for better ride control. In addition, new spring designs with lower rates and plastic liners reduced harshness. New tie rod ends and shorter pitman arms reduced friction and increased the steering ratio for easier handling. The new cushioned beam's ride delivered improved driveability.

1970 and 1971

The pickup's sales success in the seventies came on several fronts: from the serious trucker who had a hard, tough job to perform, from the city dweller who preferred a truck to a car, and from the recreational market. These diverse markets made it very difficult for truck engineers to design one truck chassis to suit everyone. Farmers, for example, wanted toughness and dependability. Camper owners wanted a smooth ride at freeway speeds with all the usual automobile amenities. Overall, we have to give truck engineers high marks because they were creative enough to fairly well satisfy the entire market spectrum. In the last two years of the Sweptline Era, Dodge engineers continued to fine-tune an already well-accepted and dependable truck.

Appearance Changes

The last new grille for the Sweptline Era (which was, in the opinion of many collectors, the finest looking of them all) was of anodized aluminum. A fresh grille always proved to give a new-truck look to an otherwise veteran body style. New side marker lights with reflectors built in served as a combined light and reflector on the front and rear fenders.

Three different instrument cluster faceplates provided distinction between the standard, custom, and Adventurer models. Provided were faceplate covers of silver and black plastic for standard interiors, bright chrome trim for custom interiors, and wood-grained faceplates for the Adventurer.

New Models

There were no new models in 1970, but one new pickup for 1971, the Sweptline Special. Built on a 114in wheelbase only, it was a lightly built pickup for the budget-minded buyer who only re-

The cab interior of a 1970 Adventurer pickup is glamorous, functional, attractive, and comfortable.

This 1970 half-ton Sweptline proudly displays its "Dude" graphics. Dudes were a tape graphics package for Sweptline pickups only. Dudes are of interest to collectors.

This extra-nice 1971 D100 Sweptline is owned by Mr. H. Christianson of Auburn, Washington.

quired a light truck. Powered only by the new 198 slant-six, the Sweptline Special was standard with a three-speed transmission, white painted grille, and black and silver instrument cluster. The Sweptline Special is of interest to the collector only because of its rarity.

The Dude Package

The only other new offering was not a model *per se*, but rather a trim package. Called the "Dude" package, it was available only on the 128in wheelbase Sweptline pickup. This snazzed-up pickup was only available for one model year, and for that reason it is also of interest to the collector.

Chapter 8

Life-Style Era Trucks 1972-1993

Dodge entirely restyled all light-duty trucks for 1972, thus creating a truck line with a new name—Life-Style. Life-Style trucks were wholly changed in appearance, in driveability, and in interior and exterior trim appointments. While the chassis was reengineered, all other mechanical components carried over with only minor updates.

Before we look further into the specifications of the new pickups, let's first examine this term *Life-Style*. The early seventies seem like ancient history now, but the most important issue impacting the pickup industry in those days was the exploding recreational vehicle industry.

The recreational vehicle industry was made up of five market segments: travel trailers, camper trailers, truck campers, motor homes, and pickup covers. Except for the motor home, all of these depended on a motorized vehicle for propulsion—in most cases a pickup, and thus a boon for Dodge. Even the motor home market helped Dodge sales:

In 1972, Dodge enjoyed 80 percent of the motor home chassis market.

Winnebago Industries in Forest City, Iowa, was Dodge's single largest customer because Win-

After eleven years of the Sweptline Era, Dodge fielded an all-new pickup in 1972. This 1972 D100 pickup is a top-of-the-line Adventurer.

Dodge awakened the sleepy pickup business in 1973 with the Club Cab, which was an immediate success. This is a 1973 D100 Adventurer.

nebago was the nation's largest producer of motor homes. By definition pickup covers and truck campers (pickup slide-ons) were 100 percent tied to the pickup market. Camper trailers were defined as the pop-up-type or collapsible tent-type trailers, and many of these were towed by pickups.

It is interesting to note that the total recreational vehicle industry grew by 35 percent in 1972 over 1971! This meant that an additional 710,200 new camper units hit the road in 1972 alone, bringing the total units in service in 1972 into the millions.

Hence, Life-Style trucking in 1972 meant, for the most part, families hitting the open road on vacation or for weekend getaways. The whole family was involved in this activity, which meant that pickup buyers were very concerned with safety, convenience, comfort, and appearance.

Recreational vehicles impacted pickups back in 1967 when for the first time in trucking history V-8 engines outsold in-line sixes. The reason was obvious—owners needed more power with which to carry or pull their recreational vehicles at interstate highway speeds. While the sixties were especially good for pickup sales, in particular from mid-decade on, pickup sales rocketed in the seventies. It took a second energy crisis and a bitter recession in the early eighties to end pickup sales increases. This chart of truck production in North America in this period demonstrates this trend:

Year	Total Truck Production
1960	1,272,051
1965	1,945,309
1970	1,967,759
1975	2,659,290
1979	3,703,767
1980	2,160,612

The early eighties were a disaster for pickup sales, but sales soon recovered and by 1985 annual production figures broke the 4 million barrier, reaching 4,309,855!

Life-Style pickups for 1972 were heavily influenced by women. Women insisted that light trucks be more comfortable and easier to drive than ever before. In 1972, 700,000 light trucks were registered to women. Other 1972 statistics of interest to pickup collectors are that 65 percent of all light trucks sold were used for personal and recreational uses, 20 percent were used exclusively for business, and 15 percent were used for both business and pleasure.

New Styling

With this background in mind, let's look at the particulars of the Life-Style pickups that Dodge spent $50 million to develop. The first element of note is its new style. The Life-Style pickup's beauty

Jerry Bougher of Oregon uses his 1975 Club Cab half-ton to pull a heavily loaded literature vendor's trailer up and down the West Coast, vending vintage auto and truck ads at swap meets. His Club Cab has more miles on it than Jerry would like to remember and has served him dependably. This photo was taken in 1988 while on a camping trip.

was new from bumper to tailgate. The massive, new, chromed front bumper, full-width grille, and broad hood gave the impression that these new pickups were fully capable of carrying or pulling RV equipment. The new rear end treatment integrated the tailgate into the side panels, and the new taillight was a wraparound design to give side visibility. The cab was wider, and curved side glass increased interior room. Doors were 2in wider and swung open 9deg farther.

New Cab

The new cab provided "Lookout Tower Viewing Power" with its curved side glass, a larger windshield for improved forward visibility, and an 8deg change in the rear window's attitude that minimized reflections. Other changes to the cab included lowering the steering column and wheel 3.25in and changing its position 14deg. The seat height was increased 2.5in and the brake pedal with automatic transmission was now the wide passenger-car-type. The restyled dash clustered all gauges and controls easily within the driver's reach. Behind the huge, padded glove-box door were located the fuse block and flasher units for convenience. The large, molded plastic glove box could be removed for access to the heater and air conditioner. The cab interior was also made more liveable through improved door and window sealing and better panel and floor insulation. Relocating the windshield wiper and heater blower motors into the engine compartment reduced cab interior noise.

Cargo Box

The wider double-wall cargo box still featured an easy-off tailgate. But as an option, **a lockable**

Adult Toys from Dodge
By Joel R. Miller

Back in the freewheeling seventies, truckers didn't want to own just any old van or pickup. They wanted to be seen in attention-grabbing, exciting trucks that put some thrills back into driving. Buyers were looking for trucks that would give them good feelings—like children at play.

Street Van

The first Adult Toy, introduced in 1976, was the exclusive Dodge Street Van. The Street Van concept was actually quite simple. Provide customers with the lowest-possible-cost, factory-built van, and then let them customize it at their own pace, based on ability and finances.

To help the owner complete his conversion easily, Street Vans came with a Customizing Idea Kit. Included in the kit were written instructions with step-by-step photos for installing porthole windows, sunroofs, roof vents, fender flares, and other accessories, plus a list of suppliers of these items. Dodge shipped each Street Van painted in one solid color, and included suggestions from Chrysler stylists to help the owner design a personalized, unique paint job. The customizing kit also contained

Bill Keyes of Alpena, Michigan, bought his 1977 Warlock new on December 12, 1977. Bill stores his Warlock from October to May, but in the beautiful Michigan summers he has logged 39,000mi. Bill has "warmed" up the 318 with an Edelbrock Performance intake and small (500cfm) AFB carburetor, Blackjack AK5000 headers, 2.25in dual exhausts, and a Mopar performance "Orange Box" electronic ignition. Bill says his Warlock's bucket seats are the most comfortable he has ever ridden on and that his Dodge is a definite "keeper."

full-size templates for cutting side panels, headliner, and floor covering for the van's interior.

Warlock

Southern California is one of Dodge's favorite locales for test-marketing new products. In order to gauge demand for a proposed new truck, Dodge dealers sold a customized, short-wheelbase D100 pickup known as the "True Spirit" in 1976. The True Spirit featured a fenderside Utiline cargo box, heavy-duty suspension, wide H78-15 tires with raised white letters, five-slot chrome disc wheels, carpeting, and a choice of seven paint colors. But what really set the True Spirit apart from the rest of the pack were its gold tape and pinstripes on the hood, fenders, doors, and tailgate.

Californians evidently approved of the True Spirit with enough enthusiasm to lead Dodge Truck marketing to include it in its 1977 line with a new name, the "Warlock."

The Warlock was identical to the True Spirit except that it was available only in six exterior colors: Black (the most common), Bright Canyon Red, Medium Green Sunfire Metallic, Citron Green Metallic, Sunrise Orange, and Canyon Red Sunfire Metallic. The Warlock's appearance was also enhanced with gold-painted spoke wheels, chrome-plated mini-running boards, and real oak sideboards. Unlike the True Spirit, which was offered only with 2WD, the Warlock was available in 2WD or 4WD versions.

Macho Power Wagon

The toughest of all the Dodge Adult Toys was the W150 Macho Power Wagon. It had just the right combination of rugged, good looks and big-bore performance. Macho it was, with a black hood, black spoke wheels, two-tone paint and striping, factory roll bar, and black front and rear bumpers. Its tailgate was painted black with large, contrasting "Power Wagon" lettering.

Unlike the Warlock, the Macho Power Wagon was outfitted with the smooth-side Sweptline cargo box. Its wheelbase, however, was the same as the Warlock's at 115in. An optional 131in wheelbase was also available.

Macho Ramcharger 4X4

Closely related to the Macho Power Wagon was the Macho Ramcharger 4X4, for those who wanted a practical, but different-from-the-guy-next-door, set of wheels. This stylish Ramcharger version combined toughness with luxury and distinctive appearance, with bold "4X4" graphics and two-tone paint schemes.

The Force

A 1978 model sold only in the West was "The Force," a replica of the 4WD off-road racing truck driven by Rod Hall. The Force featured Mickey Thompson shocks, extra-leaf front springs, Hickey roll bar and grille guard, Hella driving lights, Sears Adventurer tires, Superior wheels, front and rear trusses, floor mats, and special paint and tape stripes. All this could be had for just $1,400 over the base price of a short, half-ton 4WD.

Incidentally, Rod Hall is still winning grueling, off-road races—in a Dodge.

Li'l Red Express

The last Adult Toy to hit the street, and without a doubt the most interesting and the one that delivers the most thrilling performance, was the Li'l Red Express. It is covered in a separate section of this book.

End of the Line

The big wave Dodge had been riding was about to fizzle. One indicator that time had just about run out for the Adult Toys came in 1979. In that model year, the 400 and 440 V-8s were no longer available. The largest optional engine was the 360. Increasing federal pressure for better fuel economy was rapidly pushing high-performance out of the picture. By 1980, the

How beautiful can a collector truck be? Gary Wright of West Valley, Utah, owns this red, black, and yellow 1979 Dodge Macho Power Wagon. It is an exceptional truck. Gary's truck has only logged 46,000mi. It has a 360, automatic, black buckets, factory tilt steering, stock Goodyear Trackers, and an original AM/FM eight-track player.

Street Van, Warlock II, and Li'l Red were gone. Only the Macho Power Wagon and Macho Ramcharger survived.

Sadly, the end of the 1980 model year also marked the end for the Adult Toys. Dodge Truck took off in a whole new direction with its restyled full-size trucks for 1981.

storage compartment was now available for 8ft Sweptline pickups.

Chassis

The new frame was the drop-center-type, which lowered the cab height to allow entrance without using a step—another car-type feature women appreciated. One-ton models also had a drop-center frame. The most important new chassis feature was independent front coil spring suspension, which, when combined with wide rear leaf springs, gave a safe, firm, controlled but comfortable ride. The longer wheelbases and wider-track Dodge that engineers designed made Life-Style pickups extremely well adapted for RV use. Dodge engineers also succeeded in achieving that balance of carlike ride and handling with utilitarian load-carrying abilities.

Other mechanical upgrades included new 360 and 400 V-8 engine options; a standard 25gal fuel tank with a second 25gal auxiliary tank optional; new power disc brakes on 2WD pickups; cruise control with automatics; expanded camper packages (the Camper 7,500lb package plus new 9,000lb

and 10,000lb packages for the heavier and more deluxe slide-on campers); and a new trailer-towing package. All camper packages included a sliding rear window.

When considering Life-Style Dodge pickups, collectors should be aware of trim levels and optional equipment packages. The base level model was the custom, which was your basic "plain vanilla," no-frills work truck. Its only chromed items were the front bumper, grille, nameplate on the hood, and the model number plates on the front fenders. Even the hubcaps were painted. Its full-width bench seat was upholstered in vinyl, and the floor was covered with a black rubber mat. All other interior items, such as the doors and cab roof, were painted steel.

This spartan half-ton pickup used basic mechanicals: a 225 slant-six engine, three-speed transmission with column-mounted shift lever, and manual steering and brakes. The buyer could select either a Utiline or Sweptline pickup box.

With this as the basic Dodge pickup, a buyer then added optional equipment and optional equipment packages to suit his needs. The model

A 1979 three-quarter-ton Adventurer Power Wagon with only 18,000mi was shown at the Minnesota Collector Truck show in St. Peter, Minnesota, in August 1992. Its owner purchased it as is from the estate of the farmer who bought it new.

lineup progressed in this fashion: Custom, Adventurer, Adventurer Sport, and Adventurer Special Edition (S.E.).

1973

Ordinarily, the year following the debut of an all-new truck is a year of little or no change, especially after $50 million was spent to develop the new model. But instead of resting on its laurels in 1973, Dodge dropped the loudest firecracker ever exploded in the pickup business, introducing the revolutionary new Club Cab, the first cab-and-a-half pickup. The Club Cab was the only really new idea in a pickup's cab since the first factory-built pickups hit the streets in 1924.

The Club Cab added 18in to the cab's depth, which translated into an added 34cu-ft of secure storage space. Buyers enthusiastically welcomed this inside storage space for things an owner didn't want to leave outside in the weather.

At the outset, Dodge offered Club Cabs on D100 and D200 pickups with either 6.5ft or 8ft cargo boxes and with Custom or Adventurer trim levels only. But sales of the Club Cab were so successful that before the year was completed, Adventurer Sport and Adventurer S.E. trim levels were also added as options. A D100 or D200 Club Cab with an 8ft box rode on a 149in wheelbase chassis. With this long wheelbase and any payload at all, the Club Cab floated down the highway like a limo.

1974

In 1974, Dodge continued to build on the Life-Style theme by refining an already very successful truck. Generally speaking, these refinements are the type that makes this truck even more attractive to the collector because they either improved its appearance or added to its driving ease.

The 1980 Dodge D150 Adventurer S.E. half-ton pickup was available with either a slant-six or 318 with a fuel-saving four-speed manual overdrive transmission. The grille was restyled for 1980.

For example, under the hood the 400 V-8 was replaced by the 440 V-8 with a four-barrel carburetor for added performance in RV applications. The electronic ignition system, another industry first from Dodge in 1972, was made standard, as was an electronic voltage regulator. As a safety measure, the gas tank was moved out of the cab on all D and W models except the 115in wheelbase W100. And locking hubs were made standard on all W100, W200, and W300 models.

The collector who prefers 4WD pickups should be aware that in 1974 Club Cabs became available for W100 and W200 pickups. Trim levels for the 4WD Club Cabs were Custom, Adventurer, and Adventurer Sport only. And if your preference was for a one-ton, Club Cabs were available for D300 pickups.

Collectors should be aware of significant appearance changes such as the new grille on 1974 models. Actually, only the inner insert was changed, yet this simple change made a major impact on the appearance of the truck's front end. The only other exterior change of note was the adoption of nine new paint colors—four of them metallics.

If economy is an important issue with you, you should consider the slant-six or 318 engines. That is, of course, if you're not using your Dodge as an RV. It was in 1974 that our country was rocked by a fuel shortage due to cutbacks in supply by OPEC. The gas scare slowed pickup sales, and industry totals for the year were off by 9 percent; Dodge was down only 3 percent. Dodge countered the gas shortage problem by sponsoring a U.S. Auto Club (USAC) supervised fuel economy test in California against comparably equipped Ford and Chevrolet six-cylinder and V-8 pickups. Dodge won the 381mi test for both engine types.

1975

Improvements in 1975 were limited to engineering items rather than appearance changes with the exception of the redesigned instrument panel and interior door trim panels. The new panel presented a classy new look with its wing-shaped layout and larger cluster area, which was designed with places for optional clock, tachometer, or vacuum gauge/voltmeter combination. To improve instrument readout, a cluster hood was added to reduce glare.

Full-Time 4WD

A somewhat controversial change was to make a full-time 4WD system standard on all W100, W200, and W300 series Power Wagons. The system was designated the NP203 and was produced by New Process, a company owned by Chrysler Corporation. It had first been used in 1974 in Dodge's Ramchargers and Trail Dusters. Although Chrysler owned New Process, the system was also sold to other truck manufacturers. Both Chevrolet and Ford made the NP203 standard for light-duty 4WDs in 1975.

Chrysler engineers said the reason for going to full-time 4WD was that it made production much simpler. But automotive writers at the time criticized it, charging that full-time 4WD reduced gas mileage. That was an important criticism in this period, which fell between the first and second energy crises. Perhaps the critics were correct, because the use of full-time 4WD lasted only a few years.

Other Engineering Changes

The big block 440 V-8 was made available for all light-duty trucks, including 4WDs. This powerful option cost only $256.15 extra. Engineering made the 440 available because it was thought that its power was needed for the three-quarter- and one-ton pickups, especially 4WDs, Club Cabs, and Crew Cabs. Engine lineup then started with the 225, 318, 360, and 440 V-8s. The 400 was dropped.

All trucks with a gross vehicle weight rating under 6,000lb were equipped with a catalytic converter to meet EPA's emission standard for hydrocarbons and carbon monoxide.

Historical Note

Life-Style pickups were an instant and spectacular sales success. Sales took off immediately in 1972 and took another huge jump in 1973 due to the innovative Club Cab. The Club Cab was also a fantastic money-maker for the company. You may remember it didn't take Ford long at all to "knock off" the Club Cab with its Super Cab; Ford likes to make money, too!

1976

This was the year in which Dodge engineers corrected two "problems" that had been irritating them for several years.

The first concerned the gas tank, which protruded below the frame rails. Many questioned whether this could result in puncturing of the tank. This had not actually occurred, but the tank was lifted up between the frame rails ahead of the rear axle anyway.

The second irritant was that the pickup's cargo box had purposely been mounted a little lower in the rear than industry standards to give a more attractive appearance when less than fully loaded. When heavily loaded, however, the cargo box angled a bit toward the rear and caused many to question whether Dodge pickups were capable of carrying a load. To eliminate this situation, the

Dodge Sport Utilities 1974-1993

By Joel R. Miller

Immediately following World War II, Willys introduced a civilian version of the famous military Jeep and created an entirely new class of vehicles—the "sport utility." Combining several attributes of cars, station wagons, and 4WD pickups into one neat package, the sport utility could carry passengers and cargo just about anywhere.

The International Scout followed in 1961 and improved on Jeep's concept. The Ford Bronco and Chevy Blazer later took the sport-utility market to new heights with greater comfort and convenience.

Dodge Ramcharger 1974-1993

Although Chrysler Corporation was the poorest of the Big Three and had to watch its pennies carefully, it also kept a close eye on the sport-utility boom. The highly anticipated Dodge AW100 Ramcharger (and its clone, the Plymouth PW100 Trail Duster) finally arrived in March of 1974. The Ramcharger was sporty and luxurious, appealing to more-affluent buyers.

To cut costs and to shorten development time, Ramcharger borrowed heavily from components already found on Dodge pickups. Its off-road capabilities were enhanced by the Chrysler-built New Process NP-203 two-speed transfer case, which revolutionized four-wheeling with full-time operation. No longer was it necessary to get out of the truck to lock the front hubs before going off the road.

As a tribute to Chrysler's 4WD know-how, it's interesting to note that Chevy and Ford both used the NP-203 in the Blazer and Bronco.

Technical Highlights

The Ramcharger was built on a 106in wheelbase, with a length of 184.6in and a width of just over 79in. Available engines were the 318 (5.2ltr) two-barrel V-8, the 360 (5.9ltr) four-barrel for California, the 400 V-8 except in California, and a 440 with four-barrel carburetor. Transmissions offered were a standard three-speed manual, and optional four-speed manual or three-speed LoadFlite automatic.

How'd They Do?

Chrysler made a good showing in its first, abbreviated sport-utility model year, producing 15,810 Ramchargers and 5,015 Trail Dusters. For the full year, Chevrolet led the field with 56,798 Blazers, and Ford trailed the pack with 18,786 Broncos.

The new 2WD AD100 Ramcharger (and PD100 Trail Duster) joined the team for 1975,

The rugged 4WD Ramcharger was a new model in 1974. The rag top seen here was the only top available.

The Dodge Raider joined Dodge's sport utility vehicle line for 1987.

built on the same 106in wheelbase. It was 2.5in lower than the 4WD version. The 225 slant-six was added as the new base engine.

For 1981, better visibility was made possible with new side windows in the steel top that extended slightly over the roof. New model designators were AD150 Ramcharger and PD150 Trail Duster for 2WD, and AW150 and PW150 for 4WD versions. The slant-six was discontinued.

For 1982-1985, there were changes. The Plymouth Trail Duster did not return for 1982. Ramcharger styling carried over from the previous year. Front wheel hubs now had automatic locking.

Ramcharger production moved around 1986 from Warren, Michigan, to Lago Alberto, Mexico, when Dodge City was renovated to produce the Dakota pickup.

For 1988, the new, lighter-duty Ramcharger 100 was added. It was the value-leader with 2WD and 4WD available. The 318 V-8 was now equipped with throttle-body fuel-injection. Clutches on 4WD models were now hydraulically activated.

For 1992, the new Magnum series of engines were featured; they are covered in other sections of this book.

End of the Line

Unfortunately, after the 1993 model year, the Dodge Ramcharger was discontinued. Due to the success of Chrysler's Jeep Cherokee and Grand Cherokee, which compete in the same market segment, Chrysler could no longer justify building the Ramcharger with its slow sales pace.

1987-1989 Dodge Raider

After World War II, Mitsubishi Motors got valuable experience in 4WD with an agreement to build Jeeps under license in Japan. Later, Mitsubishi began building its own small sport-utility wagon, the Montero, in 1983. In 1987, Dodge picked up a version of the Montero and called it the Raider.

Raider's power came from a 2.6ltr (156ci) four-cylinder engine. On-demand 4WD was coupled to a five-speed manual or optional four-speed automatic. The Raider was 157.3in long and rode on a 92.5in wheelbase.

The Raider did not sell very well over its three years. Overwhelming competition just didn't warrant keeping it. The vehicle the Raider was based upon, the Mitsubishi Montero, continues to do well.

After thirty-five years the name "Power Wagon," one of the most repected names in trucks, was dropped. 4WD Dodge trucks were renamed "Power Ram." Shown here is a reskinned 1981. Side sheet metal was restyled as well as the grille and cab interior, including an all-new instrument panel.

rear suspension was adjusted to prevent the tilt under full load.

The 400 V-8 was reinstated as an option for 1976.

1977

This was a very quiet year at Dodge Truck. The only change was that the 225 became the base engine for the Ramcharger and Trail Duster sport utilities. Until this time, Dodge had maintained that sport utilities required V-8 power. But Dodge finally downgraded to the 225, as the screws continued to be turned by the OPEC nations.

Important appearance changes up front consisted of a new grille with a handsome, bold look with square surround trim for headlights and new parking lights.

A 1985 Dodge one-ton dually pickup.

1978

The truck market continued to change from the traditional demand for working vehicles to the new demand for vehicles for personal use. By 1978, almost half of light-duty trucks were purchased for personal use. People were looking for personalized fun vehicles. With that in mind, the "Adult Toys" were carried over by Dodge marketing. In fact, the exciting Li'l Red Express truck was added to the Adult Toys lineup in 1978.

Engines

One of Dodge's biggest turkeys was hatched in 1978. This was the Mitsubishi Motors-built 6DR 50A 243ci in-line six cylinder diesel, which developed 103bhp at 3700rpm. The impetus for a diesel came from Dodge dealers. Detroit was dieselizing everything in sight, including light trucks and automobiles, because of the unease regarding fuel costs. GM had its 350 diesel converted from a gas engine. Talk about turkeys; the GM diesel may have been the industry's all-time biggest turkey. At least the Mitsubishi diesel was a good engine. Unfortunately, it was too small for pickup use. Chrysler considered converting the 225 to a diesel, but the investment was too great. The Mitsubishi diesel seemed to make sense because of the strong Chrysler/Mitsubishi relationship. This small, non-turbo diesel turned out to be a stone (or a dog, skunk, or whatever your favorite term is for an underpowered vehicle). In addition, installing this engine was a real pain at the assembly plant, and it was too noisy for the van. Dodge announced that the 1979 van would have the diesel, but instead the diesel was dropped after one year. Very few were sold. The Mitsubishi diesel was installed only in D and W150 and D and W250 trucks.

The only good that came from this aborted diesel experience was that the next time Dodge engineers installed a diesel in a pickup, they hit a home run with the bases loaded with the Cummins turbo diesel in 1989. I'll get to that story further on. Dodge built 2,500 diesel-powered pickups in 1978. The diesel option in a pickup cost an extra $1,790. And it required at least 1,000mi of break-in service before it could be run at full power, which didn't set well with buyers.

The other engine development of note is that the 225 engine was made standard with a two-barrel carburetor for added performance. The two-barrel carburetor, Super Six 225, provided an additional 10hp.

Miscellaneous Refinements

Other refinements included a tilt steering column option, new steering wheels, new bucket seats for Club Cabs, and availability of Adventurer S.E. trim on all models, including crew cab and 4WD models.

Heavy Half-Tons

New 150 designations were the heavy half-ton pickups with GVW ratings above 6,000lb, the point where the most restrictive exhaust emission rules

for light trucks ran out. Because their GVWs were above 6,000lb, the 150 models needed only to meet the more liberal gasoline engine exhaust rules that applied to heavy trucks.

1979

These were dark days for Chrysler Corporation. The country's economy wallowed in a recession caused by rising energy costs and a double-digit inflation rate. Chrysler's management was in disarray, and the company was drifting like a ship with no rudder and no power. The Chrysler board brought in Lee Iacocca to rejuvenate the company. Iacocca's accomplishments are well known, so I will not rehash them here. What I do want to tell you about is the new management's impact on Dodge Truck.

It all began with what Chrysler employees called the "Boca Raton Accord." Chrysler's senior management met in Boca Raton, Florida, for some serious long-range planning well away from the distraction of everyday activities at Chrysler's Highland Park, Michigan, headquarters. The Boca Raton Accord was a decision to drop entirely out of the rear-wheel-drive (RWD) truck business by 1984. This was also when management made the decision to convert all cars to front-wheel-drive (FWD), and it was decided that they couldn't be in the FWD car business only and in the RWD business only for light-duty trucks. Along with the decision to drop out of the truck business, they made

In 1986, Dodge trucks were again warmed over with a new grille. A D250 Royal S.E. pickup is shown.

Ralph Larson of La Fayette, Kentucky, takes good care of his 1988 Dodge Power Ram W150 pickup.

This 1992 D200 three-quarter-ton cab with utility body has the restyled grille that was new for model year 1991 and continued through the 1993 model year.

a decision to disband the truck engineering group, a decision implemented immediately. This was a very, very tough time for Chrysler people, its engineers in particular. Dodge Truck engineers who retained their jobs were filtered in with the various car division's engineering staffs.

Needless to say, morale dropped into the pits. Dodge Truck drifted for several years until a truck engineering department was reestablished in 1987 with the purchase of Jeep. At that time a new enginering group called Jeep/Truck Engineering took over all responsibility for both Jeeps and Dodge trucks.

1979 Trucks

Adult Toys carried over for 1979. This was the first year for mini-pickups from Chrysler's Mitsubishi partner, the Dodge D50 and the Plymouth Arrow.

The most distinctive changes were cosmetic. The hood's center section was raised. The grille was new; it could handle either 7in round headlights or optional, stacked, dual rectangular lamps.

To meet new emissions standards, all D and W100 models were equipped with radial tires. The 225 went back to a one-barrel carburetor. A lock-up feature was added to all automatic transmissions in trucks with GVWs of 6,000lb or less. Chrysler Corporation dropped all big block V-8s, leaving only the 318 and 360.

1980

These were mighty tough days for the automotive industry. Red ink was flowing in rushing streams throughout Detroit. The watchword was survival.

Conditions at Chrysler were very tough. Chrysler had money in hand, which had been guaranteed by the federal government, but this money was to be used specifically to bring to market a new front-drive family of smaller, fuel-efficient cars. Very little was spent on the 1980 truck models. The grille was slightly tweaked, and stacked quad headlights were made standard.

Mechanical Improvements

First of all, the full-time 4WD system was now history, having been replaced by two new transfer cases: the NP208 for 4WD trucks below 8,500lb GVW, and the NP205 for 4WD trucks up to 11,000lb GVW. Both transfer cases were built with aluminum casings versus steel to reduce weight and thus improve fuel efficiency. The same transfer cases, built by New Process, were also used by Dodge's competitors.

Another interesting change was the addition of a fuel-efficient, four-speed overdrive manual transmission as standard equipment on all vans and pickups with either six- or eight-cylinder engines. The four-speed overdrive transmission was expected to deliver a 3-4 percent improvement in fuel economy over the former three-on-the-tree.

Two other changes of note included the use of galvanized steel in the cargo box to fight rust, and the availability for the first time of leather as an upholstery option (with the Adventurer S.E. option only).

Big Horn

Dodge Truck revived one of its most famous nameplates this year with the Big Horn exterior and interior trim package. The Big Horn had an intriguing, almost western look. Even though it was only a trim package, the Big Horn is rare and very attractive. It is an interesting collector truck.

1981 Dodge Ram

One could say that a new era began at Dodge Truck in 1981 because the new corporate management team had been in place long enough to make its presence felt in terms of product. The 1981 trucks were *reskinned*, an industry term meaning that redesigned sheet metal had been hung on the same veteran chassis (now in its tenth year). Ten years is usually long enough to be eligible for a new-from-the-wheels-up model. But as history will show, this tough Dodge truck platform had not even reached its mid-life yet. Life-Style Era trucks went the way of the hula hoop now that Corporate Average Fuel Economy (CAFE) restrictions, a sluggish economy, and sky-high interest rates kept truck owners at home rather than out on the interstate pulling or carrying a recreational vehicle. In fact, Dodge didn't have an engine available that could pull a travel trailer.

In place of Life-Style trucks Dodge concentrated on building Ram Tough work pickups. Durability, economy (mpg), and dull were the watchwords. No more snazzy Adult Toys or thundering 440-powered short-box half-tons. The wildest thing coming out of the Warren truck plant was a special paint job. It was a time to hunker down and survive until better days dawned to replace a miserable economy.

The New Dodge Ram Pickups

Even the names were new: Ram for 2WDs and Power Ram for 4WDs. Can you believe Dodge dropped the Power Wagon nameplate, the most respected name in trucks? Maybe it was better, out of respect to the original Power Wagon, to rename the anemic 1981 4WDs.

Not only that, but new nameplates were assigned to all models. The base model was the Custom (the only carryover). The Custom S.E. was next, then the Royal, the Royal S.E., and lastly the Big Horn. The Big Horn had all the Royal S.E. goodies plus low-back "Ram's Hide" vinyl bucket seats (a vinyl that looked like real rawhide with white fleece accents); center console; a cashmere-colored interior; gold filigree pinstripes; monotone paint in either Nightwatch Blue, Cashmere, Coffee Brown Metallic, or Black; or two-tone paint of Cashmere and Coffee Brown Metallic. The only other special interest package was the Macho truck, which began with the Royal S.E. package and also had a two-tone paint scheme of High-Gloss Black with choice of either Cashmere, Impact Orange, Bright Silver Metallic, or Graphic Yellow. (Both bumpers were painted High-Gloss Black, light-reflective tape stripe decal with "Dodge Ram" on 2WD and 4WD Sweptline tailgate in Orange and Black.) The Macho truck also included a 15in-diameter four-spoke steering wheel; 10R-15LT-B blackwall steel-belted radial tires with raised outline white lettering (installed on 15x7in steel spoke road wheels painted special Orange on 4WD models, and 15x7in radial ribbed aluminum road wheels on 2WD models); 3in-diameter sport bar (roll bar); upper and lower tailgate moldings on 2WD and 4WD Sweptline models; front stabilizer bar; carpeting on lower front door trim panel; and color-keyed side trim panel on all models.

To cap off the Ram Tough theme, the traditional Ram's Head hood ornament returned to grace the front of all Dodge truck hoods. The last year the Ram's Head had been a standard item had been 1950; the first had been 1933. Kudos to Dodge management for returning an old friend.

Engines

In those days, as now, manufacturers were required to have one set of engine specs for California and another set for the other forty-nine states, the so-called Federal specs. Except in California, the base engine was the 225 with a one-barrel, then the 318 with a two-barrel, the 318 with a four-barrel, and lastly the 360 with a four-barrel. The slant-six got hydraulic valve lifters for quieter engine operation and lower engine maintenance. The 360 was limited to trucks of 8,500lb GVW and above.

1982

The Big Horn and Macho trucks were now history, but one new model joined the light-duty lineup. An exciting truck? No, a very practical truck for the times, the Ram Miser was available only in the D150 series on either a 115in or 131in wheelbase. It was powered by the 225 teamed with a four-speed manual overdrive transmission. The Miser was engineered to deliver impressive fuel economy. Dodge engineers predicted 21mpg city and 29mpg on the highway.

1983

Another no-frills Ram Miser was added to the stable this year—the W150 4WD. It, too, was the most economical truck in its class, with a 225 six as the base engine. The Ram Misers were intended to be very basic trucks with a low purchase price. They were economical to operate, yet they were capable of doing a good day's work. Many of these

Li'l Red Express 1978-1979

What is the Li'l Red Express? "The most impressive new pickup on the market" and the "latest Adult Toy from Dodge" was the way Dodge Truck marketing announced it to dealers. This limited-production pickup's mission was to be a traffic-builder, to make profits, and to give the dealer's salespeople a conversation starter. I'll bet you thought it was for fun; no, it was a serious business decision. But, make no mistake, the engineers who put this street legal hot rod together had fun designing and engineering it.

The Li'l Red was the toughest-looking truck on the market. The competition had nothing like it. The Li'l Red was built from a basic D150 model Utiline pickup on a 115in wheelbase. It had a 360 four-barrel V-8, 3.55:1 rear axle, automatic transmission, power steering, AM/FM/MX stereo radio, "tuff" steering wheel, raised white outline-letter radial tires, and many other extras. And it had chrome everywhere—valve covers, air cleaner, vertical stacks, and rear bumper. For even more punch, it was decked out with Canyon Red paint, accent tape stripes, genuine oak panels, Adventurer trim with either red or black interior, and bench or bucket seats.

It was also well priced. Its retail price with automatic, Adventurer package, power steering, AM/FM/MX stereo radio, convenience package, oil gauge, and the Li'l Red Truck package (consisting of the 360 four-barrel engine, Goodyear GT tires, tuff steering wheel, and chrome rear bumper) was $6,244.65. Adding air and tinted glass with bench seat increased the retail to $6,840.35, and with bucket seats reduced the price to $6,424.95. Or, for those who had to have everything (that is, bucket seats, air, and tinted glass) it topped out at $7,020.65. No other options or upgrading were allowed.

One note of interest is that no spare tire was offered because front and rear wheels were two different sizes.

The Li'l Red's 360 was not your basic stock engine; rather it had some select goodies inside which gave it hot rod performance. To begin with, Dodge engineers substituted an aggressive camshaft from the high-performance parts bin. Then the stock carburetor was scrapped in place of a Carter ThermoQuad. Feeding the carb was a low-restriction air cleaner with dual fresh air inlets.

The Li'l Red's oil pan was fitted with a windage tray to keep the oil pickup well down into the oil supply. A heavy-duty version of the LoadFlite transmission with a high oil capacity valve body gave positive shifts without slippage. A high-stall-speed torque converter picked up from the passenger car's parts bin was mated to the transmission. Essentially, this engine was identical to the engine used in the Dodge Aspen Police Interceptor.

The Li'l Red was intended to be a limited-production truck. And so it was. Production was only 2,188 in 1978 (the Li'l Red was a late-in-the-model-year entry) and 5,118 in 1979. The Li'l Red may well be the Dodge collector truck of the decade!

For 1979 the Li'l Red was updated with a new grille and hood the same as the rest of the pickup line. The big change was that the engine was detuned as emissions standards were too difficult to meet with the high-performance engine. For this reason the 1978 Li'l Red is the more desirable truck. The 1978 Li'l Red is also a lower production truck and by definintion the 1978 is the original.

This original 1978 L'il Red Express was seen at the all-Mopar show in Savage, Minnesota, in June 1992.

Mel Martin of Edison, New Jersey, bought his 1979 L'il Red Express from its original owner. It has 53,000mi, original paint, and decals. Mel's truck has all the options and drives likes new.

trucks from the early eighties are still on the road and can be purchased at attractive prices. They make good everyday transportation for the collector.

1984

Again this year, no appearance changes and very few other changes showed up in the new trucks from Dodge. A little tweaking was done here and there, such as a new 15in steering wheel with new horn pad design. Power brakes were made standard on all models, an instrument panel storage box was added in the clock's former location, and key-in ignition and headlamp-on warning buzzers were added. The D150 and W150 Ram Misers were redesignated D100 and W100 models.

Dodge claimed the D100 Ram Miser was the industry's lowest-priced full-size pickup. In fact, Dodge reduced its price on the D100 Ram Miser Sweptline 115in-wheelbase pickup by $384 to a low $6,403.

1985

An historical event of note important to collectors is that the Utiline or fenderside pickup cargo box was dropped during the 1985 model year. The last production date for Utiline cargo boxes was December 14, 1984. The fender used on the Utiline dated back to 1953, unchanged in style. The Utiline was more expensive to manufacture, and its sales continued to decline to the point where it did not make sense to keep it in the line. This was also the last year for Dodge's Crew Cab pickups.

The grille, which was new in 1981, was slightly changed for the first time, although minimally. Consisting only of the addition of a thinner horizontal bar inserted between the wider horizontal bars, one has to look a second time before picking up on the change.

The major engineering change was the "Ram-Trac" front axle system for 4WD trucks. Ram-Trac featured a vacuum-actuated front inner-axle connect/disconnect system, which permitted switching to and from 4WD mode at up to 55mph by simply moving a lever.

1986

The Dodge Ram pickup was the top-selling nameplate for Chrysler Corporation in 1986. The new models were significantly improved and changed in appearance to keep the sales charts pointing upward. Dodge pickup sales had steadily moved upward from a low point set in 1980, a low point not seen since 1967. Dodge management attributed the sales improvement to better quality and value, as well as to the availability of equipment and options buyers wanted.

The world's most powerful pickup—the 1992 Dodge Cummins Turbo Diesel Club Cab Power Ram W350 4WD dually pickup.

1987

For the past two years Dodge Truck engineers had had their hands full getting the Dakota ready, first with the 2WD models in 1986 and then with the 4WD models this year. And, because of the changes to the full-size trucks in 1986, not much was new for 1987 in terms of either engineering or appearance changes.

An old friend reappeared in 1986, the Dodge Ram 100 pickup, the best full-size pickup value in America. And it was not only the best value, but also the lowest-priced in either 2WD or 4WD. Quality and value were built in.

1988

Model year 1988 was another year for engineering advancements and minor appearance and convenience improvements. The most important engineering change was a throttle body fuel injection system for the full-size truck's V-6 and 318 V-8. Fuel injection enabled both engines to increase their power outputs, which translated into better load-carrying abilities for Ram pickups. The second most important engineering change was of an historical nature: the end of one of America's finest six-cylinder engines of all time, the rugged, reliable slant-six. It was replaced by the larger 3.9L V-6, created originally for the Dakota and derived from the 318's block.

1989

The year 1989 will go down in Dodge Truck history as one of the most important in its distinguished seventy-one years as a leading truck builder. This was the year Dodge teamed with Cummins and built the most powerful pickup of all time. Here was power no competitor could touch. The story of the Dodge Cummins turbo diesel started off in a rather quiet way, but it was not long before this dynamic duo absolutely dominated the heavy-duty pickup market. The word was out: If you wanted the best, biggest, hardest working pickup, you should pick a Dodge Cummins diesel.

The Dodge Cummins was smaller in displacement than the diesels from either Ford or Chevrolet, but the six-cylinder Dodge Cummins outpulled and out-carried the V-8 diesels from the other guys. The reason was that the Cummins was a real diesel built just like the diesels in heavy-duty trucks, not the imitation carlike diesels, which was the low-priced alternative chosen by the competition. Suddenly we had a throwback to the wild recreational vehicle days of the late sixties and seventies. Dodge was now the premier pickup for towing or carrying a family's rec vehicle. Not only that, but it was the first choice for the operator who pulled or carried a large or heavy load over America's interstates.

The Dodge Ram Cummins turbo diesel was a sell-out in its first year. Dodge marketing forecast sales of 7,000-8,000 Dodge Ram Cummins diesels in 1989, but 16,750 were sold. Production for 1990 was 26,700.

The other engine news from Dodge in 1989 was that the 360 V-8 was now also throttle-body fuel injected. Another engineering change for 1989 was the addition of a new rear wheel antilock brake system as standard equipment on all Dakota and Ram pickups.

1990

Something weird happened in 1990. Dodge introduced new Club Cab models in both 2WD and 4WD trucks! What makes this weird is the fact that Dodge pioneered the Club Cab way back in 1973, but dropped out of that market after the 1982 model year. The new Club Cabs, however, were built in Mexico instead of at the Warren truck plant. The Mexican plant (where Ramchargers had been built since 1986) had continued to build Club Cabs after US production ceased.

1991-1993

1991 was the year for appearance updates. Up front was a new grille that improved the pickup's appearance considerably; this new grille style was in use for the balance of this era. Also new were new paint colors, lower bodyside and wheel lip moldings, new tailgate applique, new fabric trims, and a redesigned rear bumper for increased towing capacity.

To round out the Dodge Ram Cummins intercooled turbo diesel model lineup, the Club Cab became available in 1992. After only two years, Dodge Cummins turbo diesels had captured 25 percent of the diesel pickup market. Dodge now stood firmly on top of the high-end pickup market.

The major engineering change for 1992 was the introduction of the all-new Magnum 3.9L V-6 and 5.2L V-8 engines. These engines were not merely the old engines with new parts bolted on; rather they were almost entirely new designs with up to 85 percent of their parts being new. About the only item not changed was the basic block. Magnum engines delivered huge increases in both torque and hp outputs—45 percent for the V-6 and 30 percent for the V-8. Dodge now had the most powerful pickup engines, gas or diesel. Both new engines included sequential multipoint fuel injection systems.

For 1993, Dodge Truck management continued its quest for absolute leadership in the big-job, long-haul, daily-work-grind pickup business by converting the 5.9L (360) V-8 to Magnum power. This biggest of the Magnums put out 325lb/ft of torque at 3200rpm in light-duty cycle and 330lb/ft of torque at 2800rpm in heavy-duty cycle. Dodge Truck's slogan for 1993 was "Keep America Powerful." Don't you just love it?

Chapter 9

Vans and Small Trucks

Dodge and Fargo A-Series Compacts 1964-1970

By Joel Miller

To better understand how Dodge got into the compact truck business, it's important to recall some history. Truck makers in Europe, the Orient, and other densely packed urban areas around the world had known for many years the advantages of compact trucks. Faced with narrow, crowded streets and the high cost of fuel, foreign truck makers pioneered small, maneuverable vehicles with maximum cargo capacity.

Manufacturers such as Volkswagen gained the attention of Ford and Chevrolet, and both brought out their own lines of import fighters in 1961.

The advantages of Ford's front-engine design, its lower price, and its sales success forced Chevrolet to unveil its own new line of conventionally styled vans for 1964. The front-engine layout proved to be the way to go, and still is today.

Dodge had been planning a line of compact trucks as early as 1962. However, a few bad sales years and a massive management shakeup at Chrysler had knocked the wind out of the company. There was just no way it could afford to bring out those trucks any earlier.

Though somewhat late, Dodge was now poised to get those compacts rolling. By being forced to wait, they beat the competition at their own game. Dodge had studied several Econolines and even cut one in half to see how the Fords were made. They found the Ford well built, but Dodge felt its trucks would prove superior with more structural strength, better brakes, and bigger payload capacity.

The Dodge and Fargo A100 compact, forward-control pickups, vans, and Sportsman wagons were introduced in February 1964. Fargo models were identical to Dodge except for their nameplates; they were sold in Canada by Chrysler-Plymouth dealers. Dodge immediately took the lead in the compact van segment, a leadership role that continues to this day.

A 1964 A100 Dodge compact pickup. Its style was the same throughout its entire production run—1964-1969.

A 1964 A100 compact van.

A 1970 second-generation Dodge Tradesman
B300 one-ton window van.

A 1975 Pathfinder B300 4WD conversion.

The half-ton-rated A100s offered 213cu-ft of cargo space and a low, level floor. They had simple, no-nonsense styling and were shorter, wider, and higher than the Fords and Chevys. The Dodge compacts were 171in long, 77.4in wide, and 76.8in high. Offering a superb view of the road, the A100s had an excellent driving position with well-designed, comfortable bucket seats. Built on a 90in wheelbase with a unitized body/chassis, they had a curb weight of 3,040lb. The A100 had a standard gross weight of 3,800lb with optional GVW packages of 4,600lb and 5,200lb—the highest in the compact segment.

Two engines were offered initially—both slant-sixes—of 170 or 225ci. The 225 was the largest engine in the compact field at that time and was mated to either a standard three-speed manual transmission or an optional, dash-controlled, three-speed LoadFlite automatic.

The A100 pickup was shorter than conventional pickups but had all the cargo-carrying ability of the half-tonners. Plus, it had the desirable quality of being nimble and easy to fit into short parking spaces.

Van models could be outfitted in several combinations. The panel van didn't have side cargo doors but had a rear door with glass. The standard van had side cargo and rear doors available with or without window glass. Also, the cargo doors were available on either the right or left side.

For 1965, Dodge offered the 170 six as the standard engine, with the 225 six and a new 273ci V-8 as options. Dodge had the only V-8 in the compact field at that point and had successful sales years for 1965 and 1966.

Joining the A100 models in 1967 were the new A108 extended-length vans and wagons. At 189in long, they were built on a stretched wheelbase of 108in with 43cu-ft more cargo space than the A100. The extra length was added to the middle of the body as opposed to today's convention of grafting on a rear extension. The 170 and 225 slant-sixes were still available, and the 318 V-8 replaced the 273.

Dodge made a big sales push to move businesses out of pickups and into vans with several "Tradesman" packages. The advantages of their being roomy and offering weatherproof, secure storage were obvious. Eighteen versatile Tradesman packages were available with a wide range of shelving, cabinets, drawers, hanger bars, and partitions.

1968 was the best-ever sales and production year in Dodge's history. Over 55,000 of the new, compact trucks were produced that year, making them lifesavers for the previously ailing corporation. The A108 models proved more popular than the shorter A100 series, with almost 34,000 of the longer units built.

1969 saw the addition of a roof-mounted air conditioner on the A-Series. Van converters were having fun with the Dodge compacts. The Travco Corporation of Warren, Michigan, offered a mobile office called the "Executive Suite" and the "Host Wagon," a living room on wheels.

A100 and A108 models are still available and should increase in value modestly, particularly the well-optioned Custom Sportsman wagons. A100 pickups are the most desirable, especially with cab

---

Chrysler Minivans: Big Success with Compact Vans

Introduced in mid-model year 1984, the Dodge Caravan and Plymouth Voyager marked the return of the small van, but this time they were much more carlike than before. Chrysler's goals for the minivan were to: size it so it would fit into a normal garage or car wash, offer a low step-up and loading height, provide excellent driver visibility and easy access to all seats, and facilitate rapid conversion from a passenger carrier to cargo hauler and back.

The vehicle that emerged in 1984 was actually conceived in the Dodge Truck division as the T115 back in 1973. However, after considering the minivan at that time, Chrysler concluded that the market wasn't quite ready. Ironically, when the market was ready in 1980, Chrysler was in grave financial shape and couldn't afford to build any new products.

By 1984, Chrysler was back on steadier ground and had enough money to produce its minivan. After years of trying to beat General Motors and Ford to the punch with a blockbuster product, Chrysler had its winner and it successfully led Detroit's charge against a host of similar products from Japan. Initially, sales of the new minivans were so hot that the Windsor, Ontario, assembly plant couldn't keep up with the deluge of orders.

Traditional station wagons, with their added weight, played havoc with federal CAFE regulations, which applied only to cars. In a shrewd move, Chrysler got around the CAFE standards by marketing the minivan as a car but making it trucklike enough that the rules didn't apply.

Other minivan models introduced over the years have included: extended-length versions, the Grand Caravan and Grand Voyager (1987); the Mini Ram Van (1988) on which the standard rear hatch was replaced by dual, side-hinged, rear doors; and the luxurious, extended-length Chrysler Town & Country (1990).

New for 1982 was the 4WD Power Ram 50. This was the lightest Dodge 4WD. The 4WD Ram 50s were available in Custom or Sport series. The Sport model is shown here.

corner windows and a V-8. The Dodge compacts are very collectable, and examples in excellent condition command higher prices than comparable models from Ford and Chevrolet.

1971-1993 Dodge B-Series Vans and Wagons

Dodge's new B-Series vans and wagons were a direct response to the advancements introduced by Ford in its 1968-1/2 Econolines.

The new Dodge vans and wagons provided a larger cargo area, increased payload ratings, and outside engine access. They also included independent front suspension, longer wheelbases, and wider front and rear tracks.

Standard engines were the 198ci slant-six on the B100 and 200, and a 225ci slant-six on the B300. All models could be ordered with an optional 318ci V-8. New model designators appeared for 1971: the B100 half-ton with a GVW range of 4,200lb to 4,800lb; the B200 three-quarter-ton with GVWs from 5,200lb to 5,500lb; and the B300 one-ton with GVWs of 6,100lb to 7,700lb. 1972 was another record sales year for Dodge. A new model was added, the huge Maxivan. It was built on the 127in wheelbase and had a length of 212in. Available on the B200 or 300 chassis, the Maxivan's added length resulted from an 18in extension grafted onto the rear of the long van.

1972 saw changes in Dodge's engine lineup as the industry was forced to adapt to unleaded gasoline and stiffer emissions standards. The 198 six was dropped. The 225 six and 318 V-8 became the standard engines, and a new 360ci V-8 was optional.

Chrysler's famous electronic ignition was a new feature on Dodge vans for 1973. It provided improved engine performance, lower emissions, and longer periods between tune-ups. It was standard on B100 and B200 models and optional on the B300.

There were no major changes for 1974, except for a restyled grille and nine new paint colors. A sliding side door was added to the long-wheelbase and Maxivan models.

"Sticker shock" hit hard in 1974, with both the Middle East oil embargo and an economic recession at home forcing a downturn in sales. Fuel-efficient, six-cylinder engines suddenly made a comeback. In an attempt to help sales, Dodge supplied Chrysler-Plymouth dealers with badge-engineered versions of its Sportsman passenger van and Ramcharger sport-utility—the Plymouth Voyager and Trail Duster.

Dodge vans received a new suspension for 1976, offering a smoother, quieter ride. An improved insulation package was also available. New 400 and 440ci V-8s were optional on B200 and 300 models.

Dodge vans offered the industry's widest array of engines—from the 225 six (in all models except the B300) to V-8s of 318, 360, 400, and 440ci. Transmissions included a three-speed manual or automatic. A four-speed overdrive automatic was available on the B100 only. 1977 proved to be another good year for Dodge truck sales.

Phase Two of Dodge's van restyling started with the 1979 models. The front end was redesigned with the new, stacked, rectangular headlights; and the hood was lengthened and widened. The Maxivan was now a whopping 223in long.

Improved ride and handling was accomplished with the use of larger bushings and softer springs. The windshield received a steeper rake, which improved the van's aerodynamics and fuel economy. Safety was enhanced with a new, energy-absorbing steering column.

The optional 400ci and 440ci V-8s did not return for 1979. Continuing gas shortages and higher prices caused a downturn in sales, with sales of Dodge's vans down forty-eight percent. Dodge dropped to fourth place behind GMC. Higher federal fuel economy requirements for the car fleet led Dodge to reclassify passenger vans as trucks in October 1979. Ford and GM soon did the same.

1981 was the year of the "K-car," the vehicle that eventually saved Chrysler. On the truck side, Dodge vans were basically unchanged from the previous year. They were now called Ram vans and wagons and had new model designators—B150, B250, and B350. A new five-passenger van called the Mini Ram Wagon was introduced. It could haul up to twice the cargo of the typical station wagon.

For 1983, the B150 offered a 225 six with one-barrel carburetor and two versions of the 318 V-8, one with a two-barrel and the other with a four-barrel. The B250 could be equipped with either 318.

Dodge Street Rods, Street Machines, Hot Rods, and Customs

Historically, Dodge trucks have not been the first choice of those who prefer customized trucks. This also holds true for those collectors interested in street rods, hot rods, or customs.

A street rod is defined as a vehicle built up to 1948 and a street machine is a vehicle built from 1949 on up. Street rods and street machines retain their original style, but the owner has modernized their driveline with a newer engine and usually with an automatic transmission. Typically, these vehicles are also modernized with disc brakes, power steering and brakes, air-conditioning, and many other luxury features or modern creature comforts. Often, the vehicle's front suspension is upgraded by changing to a modern, independent suspension borrowed from a car for comfort and driveability.

Those vehicles that are changed basically only in aesthetics are called customs or lead sleds (from all the lead used in customizing the body's sheet metal). In the beginning, shortly after World War II, customs retained most of their original mechanicals with only minor changes, usually only in the interest of speed. However, in more recent years, customizers have also been upgrading their vehicles in terms of modern drivelines and mechanicals to the point that today many don't differ much from street rods and street machines. The major difference between customs and streeters is that the street owners continue to keep their vehicle's body original. Custom trucks range in age

from the late thirties to the seventies.

One truck shown here is a 1951 or 1952 customized Dodge half-ton pickup. Its roof has been lowered, parts from a Chevy car's grille have been installed in the Dodge's grille opening, all nameplates have been removed, the front bumper has been removed, and a special flame-type paint scheme has been applied.

Sydney, Australia, collector Jim Sonter spotted another street machine—a 1954 Dodge half-ton panel—at a Rod and Custom Show in Macungie, Pennsylvania, in 1991.

The panel is powered by a Chrysler Hemi with two four-barrel carbs on a chrome high-rise manifold. It appears as if everything in the entire engine compartment is chrome-plated, with the exception of the Hemi's block.

Australian Jim Sonter photographed this 1954 half-ton panel street machine. It is powered by a mighty Hemi engine.

Here is a 1951 or 1952 customized Dodge half-ton pickup with a lowered roof and plenty of customizing.

The B350 had either a 318 with a four-barrel or the 360 V-8.

1983 also would be the last year for the full-size, Dodge-based Plymouth Voyager. The Voyager nameplate would continue, however, joining the Dodge Caravan in a highly successful new line of Chrysler minivans.

A Value Wagon was added to the Dodge line-up for 1984. It was an entry-level passenger van packaged at an attractive price. Ram vans received a minor appearance freshening for 1986. The grille, bumpers, and mirrors were redesigned; and new, single, rectangular halogen headlights were added. The base van's GVW was raised to 5,000lb from 4,700lb. The industry's largest van, the B350 Maxi-van, had a GVW of 9,000lb and could handle 304.5cu-ft of cargo. A new feature on automatic transmissions was an electronic, lock-up torque converter for better highway mileage. Front stabilizer bars were now standard for better handling.

For 1987, a feature introduced years before on imported cars would find its way into Dodge vans—the "Smart Switch." Along with a new 15in luxury steering wheel, this new column-mounted stalk handled a number of functions—the windshield wipers and washer, headlight dimmer, turn signals, and optional cruise control.

Technical refinements for 1988 included a new 3.9L (239ci) V-6 that replaced the dated 225 six as the base engine. The 3.9L and the 5.2L (318) V-8

both featured low-pressure, single-point fuel injection and new camshafts with roller tappets.

A five-speed overdrive manual transmission was standard with the 3.9L V-6. Clutches were now hydraulically controlled, which allowed smoother operation and reduced drivetrain noise in the passenger compartment. The 3.9L and 5.2L engines could be teamed with the new A500 four-speed automatic, which used a lock-up torque converter and manual fourth-gear lockout.

Dodge celebrated its seventy-fifth anniversary in 1989. Its well-liked Ram Wagon was commanding a forty percent market share and continued to be a top choice for shuttle service at airports and hotels.

The 5.9L (360ci) V-8 received single-point fuel injection and other improvements that boosted power by eleven percent and torque by eight percent.

For 1992, new Magnum engines became available in Dodge conventional trucks and vans. The 3.9L V-6 and 5.2L V-8 engines were upgraded from top to bottom, with nearly every component receiving improvement. Exhaust systems were quieter and freer flowing, with a volume capacity that was eighty percent larger.

The standard engine in B150 and B250 Ram vans was the Magnum 3.9L, with a new, multi-point fuel-injection system.

1993 saw a few changes to Dodge Ram vans

The sporty 1983 Rampage 2.2 featured exterior graphics with hood scoop, fender exhauster, and side tape treatment. Standard equipment on the

Rampage 2.2 included a five-speed manual transaxle and an optional folding tonneau cover for the cargo box.

and wagons. The available 5.9L V-8 engine was upgraded to a Magnum version. All exhaust systems were now full stainless steel for long life.

From their outward appearance, Dodge Ram vans and wagons of today are virtually the same as they were when introduced over twenty years ago. Dodge never wanted to stray very far from the excellent basic design of these vehicles, choosing rather to improve them continually from technical, comfort, and convenience standpoints. This formula has worked very well for the industry's van leader in the past and should continue to do so for many years to come. When compared to Ford and General Motors full-size vans, similarly equipped Dodges are nearly equal in value. Sportsman passenger vans are considerably more valuable than Tradesman cargo vans.

1971-1972 Fargo Passenger Vans

Chrysler-Plymouth dealers in Canada sold Fargo Sportsman wagons in the 1971 and 1972 model years. Except for their nameplates, these wagons were identical to Dodge's passenger vans.

1974-1983 Plymouth Passenger Vans

Chrysler-Plymouth dealers in the US also sold an identical version of the Dodge Sportsman passenger van called the Plymouth Voyager. When the Voyager nameplate was transferred to a new minivan for 1984, Plymouth no longer marketed a full-size van.

1979-1993 Dodge D50 Compact Pickup
1979-1982 Plymouth Arrow Pickup

Chrysler had been importing the Dodge Colt subcompact from Mitsubishi Motors since the early seventies. Although these Japanese cars were well built, economical, and fun-to-drive, Chrysler never gave them much support. The company made its real money selling more expensive domestic cars and trucks that yielded higher profit margins.

General Motors and Ford had both been importing compact pickups from their Japanese partners since 1972—the Chevrolet LUV from Isuzu and the Ford Courier by Mazda. Finally realizing it also should tap this market, Chrysler expanded its sometimes strained relationship with Mitsubishi and introduced the Dodge D50 small pickup for 1979. Plymouth also offered a nearly identical truck under the "Arrow" nameplate. Ironically, just after Chrysler got into the small, imported truck market, Ford and Chevy dropped their Japanese-built trucks after 1982 to concentrate on their own domestic compact trucks—the Ranger and S-10.

The quarter-ton-rated D50 was an attractive little truck with a smooth, carlike ride and nicely done interior. Built on a 109in wheelbase with a 6.5ft box, the D50 had a length of 184.6in, a width of 65in, and, depending on tire size, a height between 60.6in and 63.4in. GVWs ranged from 4,045 to 4,520lb.

Two engines were available—both tough, torquey four-cylinders of 2ltr (122ci) and 2.6ltr (156ci). They offered Mitsubishi's "Silent Shaft" design with counter-rotating balance shafts for reduced noise and vibration. Proof of the D50's economy and range was shown by its standard fuel tank capacity of just 15gal.

For 1981, the Dodge compact was renamed "Ram 50." Three versions were now available—Custom, Royal, and Sport. The Royal offered the highest level of trim, inside and out. The Sport was the flashiest, however, with high-back bucket seats, center console, analog gauges, body side striping, and spoke road wheels.

The Plymouth Arrow minipickup would not return for 1983. The Dodge Ram 50, however, was back and rapidly gaining a reputation as one of the best compacts on the market. A new engine was offered, a 2.3ltr (140ci) four-cylinder, turbocharged diesel.

Mitsubishi had been threatening for years to develop its own dealer network because of what they perceived as an ongoing lack of dedication on Chrysler's part to adequately market its Japanese imports. That threat became a reality in 1983 when Mitsubishi gathered a fledgling group of dealers to independently sell its compact cars and trucks. This was the move that more clearly defined the love-hate relationship the two companies still have to this day.

The Ram 50 line carried over unchanged for 1984, except for the addition of auto-locking hubs as standard equipment on the Power Ram 50. Shifting from 2WD to 4WD now was as easy as flipping a switch. A new grille appeared for 1985 with a bolder "Dodge" emblem. This would be the last year for the turbo-diesel-equipped model.

For 1986, "Spring Specials" were offered, which included cut-pile carpeting, cloth and vinyl bench seat, carpeted door panel inserts, deluxe sport steering wheel, chrome front bumper, and tape stripes. Four two-tone paint combinations were available.

Dodge's small pickups enjoyed a major restyling for 1987, as Mitsubishi completely freshened them. These new compacts rated at three-quarter-ton offered a more aerodynamic look while also projecting a stocky, more powerful image.

Other improvements on the second-generation Ram 50 included better response and fuel economy in the 2.6ltr four-cylinder, a more powerful heater and air conditioning unit, and double-wall cargo boxes. 2WD models featured front coil and rear leaf-spring suspensions. 4WD versions offered protective chassis skid plates, independent front torsion bars, and rear leaf-springs. Payloads ranged up to 1,720lb.

For 1988, a new "Sports Cab" was available for all models. The Sports Cab was 11in longer than the standard cab, and it featured a short box on the long-wheelbase chassis. The extra room behind the seats provided additional, carpeted storage space.

A two-ton payload package was available on the base Ram 50 with conventional cab, long wheelbase, and five-speed transmission. It featured larger tires, power steering, and heavy-duty suspension and rear end. All Ram 50s benefited from corrosion-resistant, stainless steel exhaust systems.

New engines, a simplified model lineup, and new exterior graphics arrived with the 1990 Dodge compact pickups. The 2.0ltr and the 2.6ltr engines were discontinued. The new base engine was a 2.4ltr (146ci) four-cylinder with multipoint fuel injection.

4WD models received a new 3.0ltr (180ci) V-6. Featuring multipoint fuel injection, it produced 143hp and 168lb-ft of torque. Transmission choices with the V-6 were a five-speed manual as standard or an optional four-speed automatic with overdrive lockout.

For 1992, Dodge got back to basics by offering more competitive alternatives to Toyota, Nissan, and other small Japanese pickups. Gone were the L.E. models, the extended Sports Cab, the 3.0ltr V-6, and other long-bed Power Ram 50s.

1982-1984 Dodge Rampage Pickup
1983 Plymouth Scamp Pickup

For many years Australia was home for the unique "ute" (or coupe utility), turning out these attractive pickups with integrally styled cargo boxes grafted onto the rear of ordinary passenger cars. In the mid-to-late fifties, the Chevrolet Cameo Carrier, the GMC Suburban, and the Dodge Sweptside pickups made an attempt at looking carlike.

But let's face it, they were really just trucks wearing fancy rear ends.

Chrysler entered the car/pickup market very late with the introduction of the Dodge Rampage in mid-year 1982, and would soon realize the error in waiting so long. By then, who wanted a car/pickup any longer? The glut of Japanese pickups had satisfied the demand and practically eliminated the need for small trucks based on cars.

"Drives like a car, works like a truck" was the phrase Dodge used to introduce the T100 Rampage, Chrysler's first-ever car/pickup, and the first front-drive version offered by the Big Three. The Rampage was based on the L-bodied Dodge 024 and Plymouth TC2. The only chassis change was the replacement of the 024's trailing-arm rear suspension with a lightweight beam axle and leaf springs for the Rampage. The Rampage was built with unibody construction and a double-wall cargo box. It had a length of 183.6in, width of 66.8in, and a height of 51.8in. The wheelbase measured 104.2in, and GVW was 3,450lb. Payload capacity was 1,145lb.

The nimble little Rampage featured power front disc brakes, four-speed transaxle, rack and pinion steering, and a 13gal fuel tank. Power came from the standard 84hp, 2.2ltr (135ci), four-cylinder with a 2bbl carb.

Plymouth axed the Scamp after only one season. However, Dodge would give the Rampage one last try for the 1984 model year. Advertised as "America's only front-wheel-drive sport pickup," the Rampage received a new two-slot grille, new rectangular headlights, a new hood, and an overall appearance upgrade.

Although the Rampage was a decent little pickup, nicely appointed and available with a wide array of option packages, poor sales didn't warrant continuing it. Despite their relative rarity, Rampages and Scamps in top condition only muster values of around $3,000. Perhaps as the years go by and they become harder to find, their collector value will rise accordingly.

Chapter 10

Military Trucks and Power Wagon

★★★★★	1940 WC half-ton series with civilian styling. All body types.
★★★	WC ambulance
★★★★	WC carryall
★★★★	WC pickup
★★★★	WC command without winch
★★★★★	WC command with winch
★★★★★	WC command radio
★★★★	WC weapons carrier without winch
★★★★★	WC weapons carrier with winch
★★★★	WC weapons carrier
★★★★★	WC weapons carrier with winch
★★★★★	WC carryall
★★★	WC ambulance
★★★★	WC command reconnaissance
★★★★★	WC command reconnaissance with winch
★★★★★	WC command reconnaissance with radio
★★★★	WC knocked-down ambulance
★★★★★	WC ton-and-a-half 6WD with and without winch
★★★★★	M37 Cargo
★★★★★	M42 Command
★★★	M43 Ambulance
★★★★★	M37B1 Cargo
★★★★	M43B1 Ambulance
★★★★	1946-1968 Pickup
★★★★★	1946-1968 Pickup with winch
★★★★	1946-1968 Special bodies
★★★★★	1946-1968 Special bodies with winch

Since the end of World War II, more has been written about Dodge military trucks, including Power Wagons, than has been written about all of Dodge's civilian trucks combined. Why? I believe it is because of the way these tough, dependable trucks endeared themselves through their performance to World War II soldiers on battlefields around the world. Soldiers depended upon them for their very lives. The reputation of these go-anywhere, can-do trucks soon spread to car lovers all across the country. Many thousands of these veteran Dodge war wagons later returned to civilian life, where they again dependably performed countless tasks in industry and on farms.

Chapter one narrated Dodge's military history up to the end of World War I. We will now pick up the story from that point.

The Years Between the Wars

Dodge trucks served the Army so dependably, beginning with the Mexican affair and later in France, that they firmly established themselves in the minds of those in the Army involved with transportation. Many of these Dodge Army trucks continued in service throughout the twenties, as the country was in no mood to spend money on military equipment just after winning the war that was to have to been "the war to end all wars." At that point, the cavalry was dead—that was obvious. The question was, "What will replace the horse?" The Army knew full well that it had to find the answer to that question.

Army leaders knew they needed a light, fast, tough, and inexpensive 4WD truck. 4WD had been proven in combat in France on heavy-duty trucks, but it had not yet been tested on light-duty trucks.

In 1934 another Dodge truck made military history. This was the T9/K39x4, a ton-and-a-half 4WD cargo truck. It was the first mass-produced

This deluxe cab 1956 Power Wagon is typical of all Power Wagons, 1946-1968. Up to 1951, cargo box sides were not embossed. Power Wagons with factory-installed winches are most desirable.

The 1958 Fargo Power Wagon W300 was the same truck as the Dodge W300, but was built for export or for sale in Canada.

4WD with the modern system of front axle disconnect; axles and transfer case were built by Timken. Approximately 700 were built.

Civilian-Type Army Trucks

From a history-making 4WD, the Army next purchased Dodge 2WD trucks. In 1934 the Army purchased a quantity of half-ton 2WD civilian trucks; included were a pickup, a panel, and a wooden-bodied station wagon. These were standard production rigs with only a few minor modifications, such as a heavy grille guard.

Early Light-Duty 4WDs

In 1939, with a war going on in Europe, the Army came back to Dodge requesting several light vehicles (but heavier than the Jeep): 4WD troop, cargo, and general-purpose trucks. Dodge responded by delivering the VC Series (engineering code T202) in February 1940. These trucks were the world's first mass-produced, light-duty 4WDs. Six different body types were built, and a total of 4,641 were produced. Body types included a Command Reconnaissance, Command Radio, Closed Cab Pickup with troop seats, Closed Cab Pickup without troop seats, Weapons Carrier, and Carryall. These trucks are easily recognized by their civilian-style sheet metal.

They were followed in 1941-1942 by the half-ton 4WD WC Series (engineering codes T207, T211, and T215). They were Dodge's first 4WD Army trucks with military styling. Again, a number of body types were supplied, some with winches; a total of about 77,765 were built. Body types included an Ambulance, Carryall, Pickup, Command without winch, Command with winch, Command

The first Power Wagons with conventional cab styling were launched in 1957. The truck shown here is a 1957 half-ton. A three-quarter-ton was also built in 1957, but one-ton models were not available until 1958.

The US Navy purchased a number of these 1960 W200 Power Wagons with factory winches.

This 1961 W200 Power Wagon was the first of the Sweptline Era's tough 4WD trucks.

Radio, Emergency Repair, Panel, Panel w/radio, Telephone Installation, Weapons Carrier without winch, and Weapons Carrier with winch.

The final step in this evolutionary process was an upgrade to a three-quarter-ton chassis with a greatly reduced silhouette and wider track for better stability. These trucks were among the best vehicles built for World War II. This new design was the WC-51 to WC-64 Series with engineering code number T214. It became the standard World War II military truck, positioned between the quarter-ton Jeep and the heavier 4WD and 6WD medium- and heavy-duty trucks. Body types included a Weapons Carrier, Weapons Carrier w/winch, Carryall Ambulance, Gun Motor Carriage, Command Reconnaissance, Command Reconnaissance w/winch, Command Radio w/o winch, Telephone Maintenance, Emergency Repair, Phone Maintenance w/winch, and Knocked Down Ambulance.

If you can find a 1969 W100 Power Wagon in good condition, such as this one, snap it up; it's a highly desirable truck.

In terms of performance, quality, and dependability, Dodge's military trucks were, in a word, outstanding. One well-known Dodge military expert has said that the World War II T214 three-quarter-ton series may well be the finest light-duty 4WD trucks ever made! That's certainly a strong statement, but ask any of the army of military collectors and you'll find agreement. The performance of these trucks on the battlefields of World War II from 1942 through the end of the war cemented

The Town Wagon Power Wagon for all years is very popular with collectors. A 1962 is shown here. The Town Wagon was built on a half-ton chassis only.

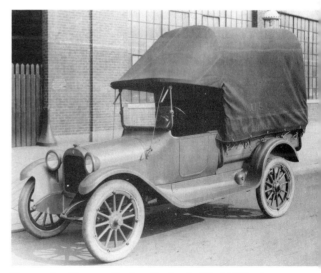

The earliest-known Dodge Brother's World War I Army truck. This is a light cargo truck with body by Budd.

Overseas Collectors

We sometimes are so provincial that we overlook what else is going on in our world. Believe it or not, we Americans have many fellow truck collectors around the world. And I am happy to say many of them choose what we like best—trucks built by Chrysler Corporation. Some of their trucks were built here and exported, and others were built overseas. These trucks may be the same as ours, or totally different, with strange names.

Do you remember the pioneer trucks in chapter one, the early trucks built by Dodge Brothers and Graham Brothers? The very first Dodge Commercial Car was actually built in England on a chassis exported from Hamtramck! And then there were those thousands of Dodge-built US Army trucks sent to Europe before Dodge Brothers sold a single Commercial (screenside) here in the US.

Chrysler has exported vehicles since the corporation was founded. The first Chrysler vehicle exported was one of the original sixes. It was shipped to Kingston, Jamaica, on March 7, 1924. The first export group was called the Chrysler Sales Corporation, which was replaced by the Chrysler Export Corporation in 1928. By 1933 Chrysler was exporting vehicles to 6,023 foreign dealers in such diverse markets as India, China, Australia, New Zealand, and South Africa. Mr. Chrysler was keenly interested in his export business and followed its activity very closely.

Collectors of Chrysler-built trucks are busy restoring and enjoying their trucks in such diverse countries as England, South Africa, Sweden, France, Israel, Australia, Argentina, Pakistan, New Zealand, Belgium, Holland, Norway, and many others. Pat Van Der Stricht, who I have known for years, is an American who lives and works in Belgium. He has his Detroit-built, 1947 Dodge WC pickup in Belgium and is very active in the European old truck hobby, enjoying every minute of it.

Coen Smit in Australia owns a 1951 DeSoto that is a very interesting truck. From the front it looks like a cross between a panel and a pick-

This 1947 Ute was built and sold in Australia. Jim Sonter

This 1936 Dodge RT was photographed at a show in London. Dwight Giles

Kees Kreling and Jan van Bodegom believe their 1946 DeSoto is the only DeSoto truck in Holland. They bought it in rough, well-used shape and have restored it beautifully in about a year.

them into the hearts of hundreds of thousands of Army and Marine Corps veterans.

Korean War Trucks

After five years of peace, the WC went back to war in Korea in 1950 to repeat its World War II heroics. In Korea, the World War II WC was joined by a new three-quarter-ton from Dodge—the M37/T245. It was an updated version of the WC/T214 series. The first M37 prototypes were tested in 1949, and production on the approved final design began in 1950. The M37 improved on the T214 in the following ways: A two-speed transfer case, which had been developed originally for the WC62 and WC63 6x6, replaced the single-speed transfer case; a quickly installed snorkel fording kit was developed; a new cab with doors and rollup windows for better weather protection was added; a new, fully weatherized 24-volt electrical system replaced the old system; a newly reengineered and improved winch of greater capacity was added; and wiring was conduited to make it more suitable for service in damp and/or dirty conditions.

Another reason for the popularity of this series is the availability of vehicles and parts. Some 255,196 World War II three-quarter-ton trucks were built. In addition, many thousands more Canadi-

The Army purchased a quantity of these 1935 light-duty 2WD Dodges. In addition to the pickup seen here, the Army also bought a double-level panel and the wooden-bodied Westchester Suburban station wagon.

A very rare 1940 Plymouth 2WD half-ton command car.

an-built trucks were exported to Allied forces throughout the world.

A unique feature of the World War II three-quarter-ton trucks is that they were designed and engineered by Chrysler specifically for World War II use. They were built "Ram Tough." All major mechanical components used in these trucks were designed and manufactured by Chrysler. These

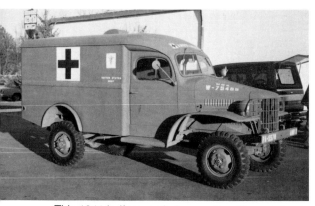

This 1941 half-ton ambulance with military styling is very rare. Only a few were built. This one was delivered to Fort McCoy in Wisconsin in December 1941. It has been restored to original Army specs even though it has only 3,100mi to date. *W. Grant Schmidt*

were not trucks assembled from components purchased on the truck parts market and assembled onto factory-built frames. They were as bulletproof as Dodge truck engineers could build them.

6WD Ton-and-a-Half Weapons Carriers

Two other highly sought-after Dodge military trucks are the WC62 without winch and WC63 with winch ton-and-a-half Personnel and Cargo trucks. These were three-quarter-ton Weapons Carriers to which a second rear-driven axle was added to produce a 6x6 rated at a ton-and-a-half. Powered by the same 230 L-6 engine, the WC62 and 63 carried 10ft bodies on reinforced frames. A major mechanical upgrade for this truck was a two-speed transfer case with a 1.5:1 ratio in low range; this was changed in March 1945 to 1.96:1.

The M37 remained in production intermittently through 1968 as contracts were received from the government. The M37 series also served with distinction in Vietnam.

Hallmarks of both the T-214 and M37 series three-quarter-ton 4WDs are that they were simple, not high-tech, trucks, unbelievably durable and tough as nails, but slow due to their low gear ratios and because they were designed for off-road use. They were easy to service and repair in the field, so they always remained in combat readiness.

The M37 was slightly more sophisticated than the WC, but not to the degree that it could be called

The Dodge WC63 six-by-six was the same basic truck as the M37 weapons carrier, but with an added driving axle and longer body.

high-tech. Models available in the M37 series were the M37 Cargo, V41 Telephone, M42 Command, M43 Ambulance, XM152 Chassis cab, and M201 Panel.

Military Collectors

Collectors of military vehicles have evolved into three basic groups set up according to vehicle size. At the small end of the vehicles are Jeeps. The next-biggest size are Dodges; and lastly are all other military vehicles, which includes everything from 4WD medium-duty cargo trucks to tanks. Certainly, many collectors of large vehicles also collect Jeeps and Dodges.

The rationale behind this breakdown is that the Jeep is the smallest, most plentiful, and least ex-

pensive to acquire, restore, maintain, and garage. Parts availability is also excellent. Dodge is next in line in terms of availability, cost, expense, and ease in storing and restoring. Parts availability is also not a problem. The big rigs are the most costly to buy and own from every measure.

1946-1968 Power Wagon

Dodge management marketed the Power Wagon in 1946 for the same reason Willys built its civilian Jeep (CJ 2A) in 1945. An unfilled niche existed in the truck market, and Dodge had a vehicle to fill it. The 1950 Dodge Truck Sales Manual makes this point.

"The Dodge Power Wagon... is without competition. No other truck manufacturer offers a

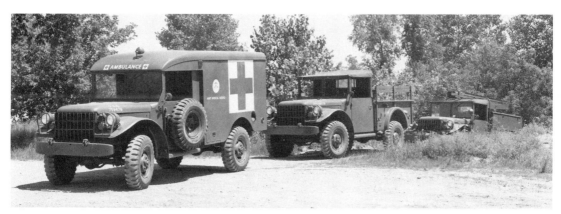

On the left is an M43 ambulance, in the middle is an M37 weapons carrier, and on the right is a V41 telephone maintenance truck.

A 1963 M37B1 weapons carrier. When I first saw this immaculately restored truck, I told its owner that it is the finest-looking Dodge truck I have ever seen! *George R. Rabuse*

model that is at all comparable. The Dodge Power Wagon was designed and built to meet a definite need. It's a vehicle built for continuous operation under extreme conditions. Its four-wheel-drive gives it tractive ability for off-the road service that would stall an ordinary truck... takes it places you wouldn't expect any truck to go."

The sales manual goes on to list seventy-five types of businesses, from airports to well drilling operations, that are prospects for a Power Wagon. Consider also that the production tooling and engineering development cost for the Power Wagon's mechanical components had already been paid for through the hundreds of thousands of World War II military vehicles purchased by the US government. Dodge had a product that did not require volume production to make a profit. The 1946 Power Wagon sales catalog proclaims on the front cover that this is "The Army truck the boys wrote home about... now redesigned for peacetime use."

The World War II WC three-quarter-ton Army truck was quickly "redesigned for peacetime use"

by Dodge Truck engineers. In 1946, the standard Dodge truck cab was the cab originally designed for the 1939 models; but somehow, when used as the Power Wagon's cab, it looked quite military. The grille, made from solid, round steel bars, and the radiator, with its external cap, were very much Army design, as were the front bumper and winch. Keeping another military styling touch, the designers chose a simple, rugged splash-guard look for the rear fenders. The running boards, rear fenders, and pickup cargo box were basically civilian issue. A rear bumper was not available. Bullet-shaped headlights perched on top of the forward curve of the fender, somewhat the same as on Dodge's conventional trucks. And of course, the tires were the deep-cleated, military type. The Power Wagon sat quite tall due to its large tires and the fact that it was a 4WD. Nevertheless, the front axle and differential were not in full view.

Dodge constantly emphasized that the Power Wagon was unique due to its 4WD capability. Equally emphasized was its ruggedness, which made the Power Wagon at home off the road as well as on. Dodge marketed the Power Wagon on these premises: The customer could use it for *Pulling Power,* in place of a tractor pulling a plow; for *Portable Power,* as in running a saw; or for *Carrying Power,* as in a pickup hauling a load. The Dodge salesman's challenge was to convince customers to create jobs for the Power Wagon to handle. The sales literature urged, "Its usefulness is restricted only by the ingenuity of the owner!"

The Power Wagon was originally available as a pickup, chassis cab, chassis with windshield cowl, and chassis with flat-face cowl In later years it was available only as a pickup, chassis cab, and chassis cowl.

Power Wagons are highly sought-after. The front-mounted winch is a very valuable accessory. Power Wagons with aftermarket bodies, such as a small school bus, a wooden-bodied station wagon, and other specialized bodies, are available and make interesting collector vehicles. Vehicles and parts are in generally good supply at reasonable prices.

Chapter 11

Plymouth Commercials 1930-1941

By Jim Benjaminson

★★★★ 1930-1931 30U
Commercial Sedan
★★★★ 1935-1942 Commercial
Sedan
★★★★ 1937 PT50 pickup and
station wagon
★★★★ 1938 PT57 pickup and
station wagon
★★★★ 1939 PT81 pickup and
station wagon
★★★★ 1940 PT105 pickup and
station wagon
★★★★ 1941 PT125 pickup and
station wagon
★★★★ 1939-1941 Roadking
utility sedan

"I never knew they made such a thing." It's a phrase heard virtually every time a Plymouth "Commercial Car" is seen, whether at an antique truck meet or on the street. Yet for five years, Plymouth did build and market its own line of light-duty trucks. Looking back over half a century, it makes one wonder why Plymouth didn't build a truck sooner—or build it longer. Yet in some respects you may have to wonder why they built one at all.

Between 1930-1942, Plymouth built a confusing array of commercial vehicles, utilizing both passenger car and truck chassis. Regardless of the platform on which they were built, these commercial offerings were never produced in large numbers and have virtually gone unnoticed by hobby collectors.

Passenger Car Chassis

For the sake of clarity, we will examine the commercial offerings based on passenger cars first.

Plymouth's first entry into this market came with the 30U models, built in 1930-1931. Called the "Commercial Sedan," this was little more than a two-door sedan with a third door added at the rear of the body. The rear quarter windows were blanked out with removable panels (usually these panels carried the name of the business on them). The idea behind the Commercial Sedan was to serve two purposes for the small businessman who could afford only one vehicle. During the week, the sedan could be his delivery truck; but on the week-

Frank Schreckenberg of Faribault, Minnesota, owns this very rare 1935 Plymouth PJ commercial sedan. It has a large sedan delivery-type rear cargo door. Plymouth's PJ commercial sedan was converted fom a two-door passenger car.

Donald Idarius of Chicago provided this 1940 photo of his 1937 sedan delivery. He said, "I drove this tough little panel truck in 1940—coincidentally, my personal car was a 1937 Plymouth coupe. I used to load this truck down with pipe, conduit, cable, heavy construction tools, and so forth for delivery to job sites in the Chicagoland area. It was rugged and dependable as well as speedy and responsive."

A rear view of a 1937 Plymouth sedan delivery. This immaculate, fully restored truck was photographed at the 1988 Plymouth National Meet in Plymouth, Michigan.

end, with the window panels removed and the optional rear seat in place, it served as the family car. As a passenger vehicle, even while in the commercial mode, it easily traveled in restricted areas where "commercial vehicles" were prohibited. Despite the obvious advantages, the Commercial Sedan met with little sales success; in fact, only eighty were built. At $750 (later reduced to $675), it was considerably more expensive than the $565 two-door sedan on which it was based, which may account for its low sales volume.

The Commercial Sedan did not reappear in the Plymouth sales lineup until 1935. Again it was based on the lowest-priced two-door sedan, with a third door cut into the rear of the body. Although 1935 bodies were of all-steel construction, the rear door was framed in wood. The rear seat was optional for those wanting to convert from commercial to personal use. Snap-in window blanks were used to advertise the name of the business. With

the window blanks removed, the rear quarter windows could be rolled down. Built by Briggs, the $635 Commercial Sedan (body code number 651-B) was only $100 over the cost of the regular PJ Business two-door sedan (body code 651) on which it was based. Sales of 1,142 Commercial Sedans no doubt reflected this price difference.

For 1936 Plymouth built the Commercial Sedan with its own special body rather than converting a two-door sedan. Based on the P1 "business" passenger car chassis (from 1935 through early 1938 Plymouth would always refer to its lowest-priced models as "business" models), prices were reduced $20 over the previous year as sales climbed to a record 3,527 vehicles. The quarter window panels were now permanent, and no rear seats were offered to convert the sedan delivery to passenger car use. Like the 1935 version, this sedan had a single door at the rear of the body, while the spare tire was carried in the right front fender. The gas filler pipe was curiously located inside the rear compartment—making it necessary to open the back door to fill with gasoline.

A major change occurred with the 1937 Commercial Sedans (it will be covered in more depth in the Commercial Car section of this chapter) when it was decided to build this model on the truck chassis. The wooden-bodied station wagon was also shifted to the truck chassis (it had been based on a passenger car chassis previously but had still always been considered by the factory as a "commercial" car). The only "commercial" vehicles on the passenger car chassis in 1937 were the ambulance/hearse conversions and pickup box options.

For 1938, the sedan delivery (or Panel Delivery, as Plymouth preferred to call it) remained on the commercial chassis, while the wooden-body station wagon returned to the passenger car chas-

The 1937 Plymouth PT50 was the first truck-built Plymouth commercial. This new Plymouth was a badge-engineered Dodge pickup. *Vernon Meyer*

The 1939 Plymouth sedan delivery's style, including flush headlights, was new in 1939 and identical to that of Plymouth cars.

sis. As in 1937, the ambulance conversion and the removable pickup box were offered on the P5 Business/Roadking chassis.

Plymouth Commercial Cars for 1939 were built on a new, truck-type, 116in wheelbase chassis, which may explain why the Panel Delivery once again reverted to the passenger car chassis. Though designed to match the passenger car line, the Panel Delivery, Utility Sedan, and station wagon differed from the passenger cars in that they carried their spare tire in a side-mounted fender well. The Panel Delivery still had its own special body; only now it had two doors, split vertically, at the rear of the body. Each door contained its own retractable window, fitted with flush-mounted handles to eliminate the possibility of scratching the merchandise.

Joining the lineup this year was a new "Utility Sedan." Like the Commercial Sedans of 1930 and 1935, the Utility Sedan was a converted two-door passenger car built without a rear seat. The partition between the passenger compartment and trunk was eliminated, as in the ambulance conversions (which were now offered in either the P7 Roadking or P8 De Luxe touring sedan bodies). Below the window, paneling replaced upholstery, while the floor was covered with a full-length rubber mat. Unlike the Panel Delivery, which came with only a driver's bucket seat (passenger side optional), the Utility Sedan was shipped with two bucket seats. An optional screened partition with

locking gate was offered to separate the driver from the load compartment of the Utility Sedan. Only 341 of the $685 Utility Sedans were sold, in comparison to 2,270 of the $715 Panel Deliveries.

Plymouth's 1940 passenger-based "commercial" offerings also included the Utility Sedan and the Panel Delivery on the P9 Roadking chassis (although one P10 De Luxe chassis Panel Delivery was built for a Detroit area radio station). Styling imitated the passenger cars on which they were based, the Utility Sedan being a stripped two-door sedan, while the Panel Delivery again had its own special body.

The body styles based on a two-passenger car were continued into 1941. At $739, the Utility Sedan fell to sales of 468 units. Sedan delivery production rose slightly, to 3,200, as did the price, to $745. Despite slowly increasing sales, the Panel Delivery was not offered in 1942, although the limited-production Utility Sedan was. Also missing from the 1942 lineup was the ambulance conversion—1942 was the last year for any passenger-based Plymouth commercial. Like the 1930 Commercial Sedan that had started the whole program, the 1942 Utility Sedan saw only eighty units built.

The Commercial Car Chassis

Why Plymouth chose to enter the commercial market in 1937 may have more to do with the structure of the Chrysler Corporation than anything else. Plymouth was one of the "Big Three"—

The 1940 Plymouth PT105 pickup is a favorite with collectors due to its exceptional beauty.

Chevrolet, Ford, and Plymouth—ranked according to their sales status. Both Chevrolet and Ford marketed a complete line of commercial vehicles, from light- to heavy-duty. But was there really a need for another member in the already burgeoning truck market? When it came to trucks, the big three were Chevrolet, Ford, and Dodge—so why another truck line from Chrysler? Again, it all stems from the corporate structure mentioned earlier.

When first introduced, Plymouth was the "exclusive" offspring of the Chrysler Division. In 1930 Walter Chrysler wisely saw fit to dual Plymouth with all Chrysler, Dodge, or DeSoto franchises. During the height of the Depression years, when it was difficult to sell even the least-expensive automobile let alone the more expensive models, it was Plymouth that helped keep many of these dealers in business. This dualing resulted in Chrysler-Plymouth, Dodge-Plymouth, and DeSoto-Plymouth dealers. Those Plymouth dealers dualed with Dodge had no problem when it came to servicing accounts that needed commercial vehicles. But for those who were DeSoto-Plymouth dealers, the story took on a completely different slant. They may have had the market—but not the product.

In Canada, too, the corporate structure, although different from that in the United States, eliminated a great number of dealers from participating in the growing truck market. Complaints about this situation did not fall on deaf ears in the Highland Park corporate offices. Chrysler Corporation could, with little expense, easily build a companion line of trucks for both the US and Canadian markets. Dodge would provide the basis for both, although each of the companion marques would enjoy its own identity.

By 1936, Canada had its Fargo line, while Plymouth dealers would have to wait one more year for a Plymouth Commercial Car. No explanation was ever given as to why the Canadian Fargo (and US-built Fargos for export markets) were offered in all models and tonnage ratings, while Plymouth was restricted to light-duty models only.

1937 PT50

Production of the new Plymouth Commercial Car line began in December of 1936. Plymouth's first truck-type pickup was little more than a disguised Dodge pickup. All-new for 1936, the Dodge was "updated" for 1937—it and the "new" 1937 Plymouth pickups were virtually identical except for minor trim differences such as the grille and tailgate. The Plymouth pickup used a Plymouth engine, coded series PT50 by the factory. (Dodge

The 1941 Plymouth PT125 pickup was the last Plymouth pickup until the eighties.

trucks were coded series "T"; Plymouth thus became "PT" for "Plymouth Truck" to indicate the heritage).

Built on a 116in wheelbase ladder-type frame with five crossmembers, the new Plymouth "Commercial Cars"—as they were called by the factory—bore a strong resemblance to the passenger cars. The resemblance was in looks only, though, as no sheet metal or trim interchanged between the 1937 passenger car and 1937 truck, with the exception of the front bumper, hubcaps, and dash knobs. (Some items, such as the rubber-covered running boards and front fenders from the 1936 passenger car, will interchange with some minor modifications.) Unlike Dodge, which offered a complete line of models, Plymouth offered Commercial Cars in just four versions—the Express (pickup), Chassis Cab (which included full-length running boards and rear fenders), Panel Delivery, and station wagon. A flat-face cowl could also be ordered by those who wanted to mount a special body.

1937 would be the only year the wooden-body Westchester Suburban station wagon would ride on the PT50 truck chassis. It should be noted that the wagon body was not built by Plymouth, but rather by the U.S. Body & Forging Company of Tell City, Indiana. Bare chassis were shipped to Indiana, where the bodies were fitted. The completed units were shipped back to the factory for final shipment to the selling dealer.

Attractively styled, the PT50 series included safety glass in windows as standard equipment. A chrome front bumper was also standard, with a rear bumper available as an option. (Rear bumpers were standard, however, on Panel Deliveries.) The spare tire on the series was mounted in the right front fender. A left fender well was available at extra-cost. The pickup box was 6ft long and 47.5in wide, just a half-inch short of carrying a 4ftx8ft sheet of plywood. The box of the PT50 and PT57 pickups were all-steel construction, including the floors.

Under the hood sat a familiar valve in a block, six-cylinder engine. With a bore of 3 1/8in and stroke of 4 3/8in, it displaced 201ci—the same as for Plymouth passenger cars from 1934 through 1941. The truck engine was rated at 70hp at 3000rpm, while 1937 passenger cars were rated at 82hp. A 10in clutch coupled to a three-speed, and a floor shift transmission transmitted power to the semifloating, hypoid rear axle. Standard axle ratio was 3.73 with optional ratios of 4.1:1 or 4.78:1.

The Panel Delivery, which up to this time had always been on the passenger car chassis, was now part of the commercial chassis lineup. Priced $50 higher than the previous year, the Panel Delivery found 3,256 buyers.

The 1941 Plymouth sedan delivery was based on a passenger car. This beauty has been totally restored.

1938 PT57

Plymouth's 1938 Commercial Cars were so little changed, except for minor adjustments to appearance, that the lines shut down for less than a day for model year changeover.

While 1937 had been a boom year, 1938 turned out to be a year of severe recession after several years of improvement in the economy. Not helping the situation any was a price hike. In addition, dealer lots were full of used cars and trucks that could be purchased for less than new. By year's end, Plymouth and the entire auto industry found sales slashed nearly in half compared to 1937. In retrospect, 1938 auto sales were only slightly better than they had been during the Depression years of 1931 to 1933!

The PT57 continued to be built at the same three assembly plants. Production of the PT57 models came to a halt on August 17, 1938—year-end totals—4,620 pickups and ninety-five chassis cabs. Despite the drastic drop in sales, Chrysler continued constructing a new truck plant, which opened in October of 1938. Located on Mound Road in Warren, Michigan, the plant was said to be the world's most modern plant dedicated to the exclusive manufacture of commercial vehicles.

1939 PT81

When Plymouth unveiled its new Commercial Cars for 1939, things had definitely changed. Gone was the "I'm almost a passenger car" look. The new pickups had a decidedly trucklike appearance. These trucks were all-new except for engines, and the wheelbase remained at 116in.

The new cab was moved forward, as was the engine, to provide for a cargo box that was 6.5in longer without drastically increasing the outward dimensions of the vehicle. The cab had a more modern look, with a front end like a ship's prow, headlamps mounted on the fender catwalks, and a two-piece, V'd windshield among the more noticeable changes. The cab was the biggest offered by the "Big Three" and was advertised as a true "three-man cab." The box was increased in size, measuring 78 1/8in long by 48 1/4in wide (now wide enough to carry a 4x8ft sheet of plywood flat on the floor!), while the sideboards rose to 14 3/8in before meeting the flareboards. Departing from the all-steel boxes used in 1937 and 1938, the new box had a wooden floor, made up of 13/16in, thick oak planking protected by steel skid strips.

Other exterior changes included more-massive fenders, each featuring four prominent "speed lines." Fender-mounted spare tires were eliminated—the spare now rode in a special carrier under the box at the rear of the frame.

Outside of the sailing ship hood ornament, headlamp rings, and hubcaps, no bright metal trim appeared on the new models. Even the front bumper, which had been chrome-plated on the 1937-1938 pickups, was now painted black. The windshield frame, headlamps, and entire radiator shell could be finished in chrome at additional cost, but few were so equipped.

Mechanically, the PT81 series differed little from its predecessors. The engine remained a 70hp,

This 1956 Powell station wagon belongs to David Sams of Eureka, California. The round devices seen in the rear view are special holders for fishing poles. This wagon is very rare and highly desirable. Production of both body types only exceeded 800 total units for the entire two-year production run, 1955-1956.

201ci six, with three-speed manual transmission standard and four-speed optional. The radiator was increased in size, front springs were increased in length from 30in to 36in, while a wider rear axle increased rear tread to 60in.

Only two assembly plants built Plymouth's 1939 Commercial Cars—Detroit and Los Angeles. It should be noted that with the exception of the sheet metal between the front fenders, Dodge and Plymouth cars were virtually identical. Dodge used a two-piece (upper and lower) radiator grille, while Plymouth and Fargo used a three-piece radiator grille (a one-piece, vertical center surrounded by left and right lower grilles).

Built from September 1, 1938, through August 31, 1939, the PT81 saw a modest increase in production to 6,181 pickups and 140 chassis cabs. These figures would set a sales standard that would remain nearly static for the rest of the Plymouth truck's production life.

Military Plymouth Pickup

Some 1940 PT105 trucks had the spare tire mounted above the running board forward of the right rear fender. These trucks have a special indent in the rear fender to allow this type of mount, with the mounting arm attached to the frame and passing through an opening in the running board splash apron. These trucks also had the gasoline tank mounted at the rear of the frame instead of under the seat. The gas tank filler neck was located on the left rear fender instead of at the cab sidewall.

1940 PT105

The 1940 series PT105 had only minor appearance changes. The new truck went "on line" August 15, 1939—while trucks were still being built to 1939 specs. New for the year was the addition of sealed-beam headlamps, replacing the old bulb and reflector type of years past. With the change to sealed beams, it was no longer possible to mount the parking lamp in the headlight bucket. There were a few subtle changes in the mechanics of the PT105 series—horsepower was increased from 70 to 79; torque was also increased, but bore and stroke figures remained the same. The switch to sealed-beam headlamps mandated the use of a larger 35amp generator. A floating-type oil pickup with screen, fuel filter at the carburetor, and cross-and-trunion propellor shaft U-joints rounded out the changes.

Last but not least was the switch to left-hand and right-hand thread wheel bolts. Plymouth continued to use wheel bolts rather than studs pressed into the brake drums. To ease the problem of getting a wheel into place, brake drums had a guide

118

stud attached to them. A corresponding hole in the wheel was slipped into this guide to properly position the wheel.

1941 PT125

Despite only minor changes between the 1940 and 1941 Plymouth Commercial Cars, the PT125 did not go "on line" until September 18, 1940, better than two months after shutdown of the PT105 series. Most of the changes were for the better, although the most obvious change—moving the headlamps from the catwalk to the crown of the fender—was a change for the worse in the opinion of many.

Without making any changes to the basic radiator sheet metal, Plymouth designers fashioned a chrome overlay patterned after the 1941 passenger car grille. Starting at the leading edge where the hood meets the radiator shell, a stainless strip ran forward to converge at the front of the radiator. From there it plunged down in two vertical strips to the bottom of the grille shell. In the center was a large Plymouth sailing ship emblem. On either side of this, on the left and right outer grille panels, were five horizontal stainless strips, similar to the strips used on the 1939 and 1940 Plymouth passenger cars. Paint stripes accented the bars between the stainless strips. The front bumper had a distinctive V at its center.

Under the sheet metal were a few changes, most notably a higher-horsepower engine with increased torque (82hp vs 79hp in 1940), a new three-speed synchroshift transmission, and an oil-bath air cleaner—all standard equipment. Also new for the year were stepped brake cylinders with different size pistons in the same cylinder. Front pistons measuring 1 1/4in actuated the front brake shoes, and rear pistons measuring 1 3/8in actuated the rear shoes. This difference in size—or stepping—was claimed to exert equal pressure by both shoes.

As production wound down on the PT125 models, so too did an era at Plymouth. With the dawn of the 1942 models, the Commercial Car line was quietly dropped. The reasons why were never publicly discussed. No doubt lower-than-expected sales volume was a factor. A more plausible explanation probably lies in the commitments made to the military to supply trucks for the war. Although Plymouth truck production had halted prior to our entry into World War II (unfortunately no one recorded the date), it was obvious Dodge was going to need all the production facilities it possessed to build the varieties and quantities of military vehicles needed by our allies and ourselves. Civilian truck production came to a halt on April 30, 1942, as Chrysler helped turn Detroit into the "Arsenal of Democracy."

Plymouth Commercial Car Identification Data

Plymouth Commercial Car serial numbers can be found on a plate riveted to the right front door post on all models. In addition, a body code plate is located on either the right front door post or directly above the steering column on the engine side of the firewall. Plymouth engine numbers are located on a flat boss on the left side of the block, directly above the generator. Engine numbers are coded to include the model series as well as a sequential build number. The engine code may also include additional information following the sequential serial number; it indicates a factory engine fitted with oversize or undersize parts according to the following code. The letter *A* indicates a .020 oversize cylinder bore; *B* indicates .010 undersize main and connecting rod bearings; and *C* denotes .005 oversize connecting rod bearings. The letters *AB* together indicate both a .020 oversize bore and .010 undersize rod and main bearings. The letter *E* indicates an "economy" engine with a small bore carburetor, while some export models may have the letter *X* following the model code, indicating a small-bore engine sold in certain overseas export markets.

1937 PT50 Serial Numbers
Detroit 8850101 to 8861664
Los Angeles 9206601 to 9208113
Evansville 9182701 to 9185187
Engine Numbers: PT50-1001 on up
Body Code Numbers: Start with K-8-2-LR

1938 PT57 Serial Numbers
Detroit 8618701 to 8624135
Los Angeles 9208201 to 9208797
Evansville 9185301 to 9186416
Engine Numbers: PT57-1001 on up
Body Code Numbers: Start with K-8-2-LR

1939 PT81 Serial Numbers
Detroit 8624201 to 8630418
Los Angeles 9208851 to 9209340
Engine Numbers: PT-81-1001 on up
Body Code Numbers: Start with M-1-2

1940 PT105 Serial Numbers
Detroit 8631001 to 8637730
Los Angeles 9209351 to 9210053
Engine Numbers: PT105-1001 to PT105-34654
Body Code Numbers: Start with 4012-*****

1941 PT125 Serial Numbers
Detroit 81000101 to 81006107
Los Angeles 9210101 to 9210700
Engine Numbers: PT125-1001 on up
Body Code Numbers: Start with 4112-*****

★★★★	1989-1990 Shelby Dakota V-8 pickup
★★★	1989-1990 Dakota Sport Convertible pickup

Dodge Dakota 1987-1993

The Dodge Dakota was much more than the world's first, true, midsize pickup. It represented the "New Industrial Revolution" at Chrysler Corporation. The Dakota didn't just happen. Before it came about, a new, high-tech assembly plant was needed in which to build Dodge's most high-tech pickup.

When Dodge Truck's Warren, Michigan, assembly plant was completed in 1938, it was heralded as the most modern, efficient, and largest exclusive truck assembly plant in the world. In the years since, millions of high-quality Dodge trucks have passed through its doors. Because the unique new Dakota demanded the most advanced manufacturing technology available, the old Warren plant was totally modernized at a cost of $750 million. It also

got a new name—"Dodge City." The complex was equipped with sophisticated new production equipment and conveyers, robotics, a greatly expanded computer system, and everything else needed to assemble the best trucks possible. Dodge City builds both the Dakota and full-size trucks. Components are supplied by Chrysler's Mound Road engine plant and Warren stamping facilities, which feed parts directly into Dodge City, along with engineering and technical support from the nearby Outer Drive Technical Center.

An additional 144 acres, adjacent to the original site, were purchased to build a new paint facility. It houses advanced robotic equipment to assure a world-class finish.

Dodge management brought the world's first midsize pickup to market late in 1986 as a 1987 model. This photo was taken in September 1986 outside the main gate at Chrysler Corporation's Highland Park, Michigan, headquarters.

Dodge was the official truck for the 71st Indianapolis 500 race. Full-size pickups were used at Indy in addition to this short-wheelbase 4WD V-6 Dakota pickup.

The Midsize Dakota

The Dakota represented an investment of over a billion dollars by Chrysler. In addition to the $750 million spent to create Dodge City, another $300 million went toward designing the Dakota.

The biggest compliment one can pay the Dakota is that it is the truck GM and Ford wished they had built instead of their own compact trucks. Sooner or later, they will have to spend the money to develop their own midsize trucks. The decision to proceed with a midsize truck, or the N-Truck as it was called during the design and development stage, was made in 1983. At that time, it was going to be a joint venture with Chrysler's Asian partner, the Mitsubishi Motor Corp. As it was planned, the N-Truck at 1,700 millimeters (mm) was too wide to be of interest to the Japanese because their government's regulations would have placed it in a higher tax bracket. Nevertheless, the proposed truck looked so good to Chrysler's senior management that they allowed Dodge Truck to go it alone.

Remember that at this time Dodge Truck did not have a dedicated truck engineering staff, so they were required to go outside for engineering and development help. Carron and Company of Dearborn, Michigan, was chosen for the N-Truck project. Carron is an engineering job shop and prototype builder. It was able to focus exclusively on the project and consequently had models running in record time. The decision to build the Dakota was made in 1983, and the new truck was introduced on October 2, 1986—a record for Chrysler.

Niche Marketing

Extensive research revealed that many pickup buyers wanted a truck with less bulk than a full-size model, but more room and muscle than either the imported or domestic small pickups offered.

Thus, the unique Dakota was positioned between the full-size and small trucks. It was designed with either a 6.5ft cargo box on an 111.9in wheelbase or an 8ft cargo box on a wheelbase of 123.9in. Another definite advantage was its three-man-wide cab. An available, muscular V-6 engine could handle a 2,550lb payload, and several appearance items could be added to provide a sporty, personal transportation look. Rack-and-pinion steering was a first for Dodge and for the US truck industry.

Dakota Engines

The Dakota's engine compartment was designed for easy servicing. Carefully routed wiring harnesses and vacuum lines eliminated congestion and confusion. There was plenty of work room in the engine bay, and spark plugs, wires, and fuel and oil filters were all easy-to-reach.

The base engine was the corporate 2.2ltr four-cylinder mounted longitudinally. Bosses were added to the 2.2's block casting for motor mounts to allow the engine to be turned 90 degrees from its usual transverse orientation. Carburetors using electronic control of fuel-air ratios with oxygen feedbacks minimized exhaust emissions.

The Dakota 2.2 used the same fast-burn cylinder head, valve gear, and valve cover as the passenger car version. The oil pan and oil pickup were redesigned to clear the front frame crossmember, but accessory mounting brackets on the right side of the engine were unique to the Dakota. The 2.2ltr engine was mated to a five-speed manual overdrive transmission.

In 1989, the Dodge Dakota Sport Convertible was the only factory-built rag top pickup.

The 1991 Li'l Red Dakota Express was an after-market conversion emulating the 1978-1979 half-ton Li'l Red Express.

3.9L V-6

Chrysler engineers took the tried and true 318 (5.2ltr) V-8 and built a 3.9ltr (238ci) V-6 from it for the Dakota. The V-6 was made by sectioning the 318's block, removing the back half of the front two cylinders and the front half of the next two. This arrangement provided excellent performance and reduced engine imbalance.

The carbureted 3.9ltr produced 125hp at 4000rpm and delivered a peak torque of 195lb-ft at 2000rpm. Compression ratio was 9.1:1.

The 3.9ltr V-6 was built on the same engine line as the V-8s and was designed for maximum interchangeability of components. Most engine accessories were common to both.

This bright red 1991 Dodge LRT (Little Red Truck) was a Concept Pickup Truck built up from a Dakota pickup. This truck was the second one of its type. The original LRT's style was so close to the style of the future T300 Dodge Ram pickup that Chairman Lee Iacocca ordered it pulled from the car show circuit. *Elliott Kahn*

Transmissions available with the V-6 included a five-speed manual or a three-speed automatic. Clutches on Dakotas with manual transmissions were hydraulicly activated.

1987

The Dakota was launched in 1986, but was considered a 1987 model. The new midsize truck included a windshield raked at 48.5 degrees and flush-mounted for improved aerodynamics. Level floor and door sills provided increased ease of entry. The Dakota's body was designed with a minimum number of separate body panels and welds to increase structural strength and durability.

Later in the model year, rugged 4WD versions were added to the lineup. Special features of the Dakota 4WD included independent front suspension, standard power brakes and steering, 15in wheels and tires, and a New Process NP-207 "Ram Trac" transfer case. The Dakota was the first Dodge-built 4WD to use an independent front end with torsion bars for a quiet, comfortable ride, both on and off road.

1988

The new Dakota Sport joined the model lineup for 1988. The Sport version was available in 2WD or 4WD; it featured unique exterior graphics for buyers seeking personal transportation that could double as a work truck.

The Dakota V-6 was fuel-injected for 1988 and was the standard engine for 4WD and Sport models. A new four-speed automatic replaced the original three-speed for increased fuel economy.

1989

This was an exciting year for Dakotas. The Dakota convertible debuted as a Spring Special. Chrysler, the leader in the revival of the convertible car, decided a drop-top truck might also be a winner. A small number of completed 2WD and 4WD Dakota Sports were shipped from Dodge City to a nearby ASC, Inc., plant for conversion.

The Dakota convertible was a result of favorable reviews from the automotive press, Dodge dealers, and auto show crowds. Convertible trucks produced by small shops had gained in popularity, especially on the West Coast, but Dodge's answer was the first, recent production convertible truck attempted by a major manufacturer. The Dakota Sport convertible was available in just three colors: red, black, or white.

Another new model for the spring came out of Whittier, California. It was the limited-distribution Shelby Dakota, featuring a 5.2ltr V-8 and four-speed automatic. Carroll Shelby, famous for his high-performance muscle cars of the sixties, returned to the game—this time with a truck. Along with the big engine, the Shelby Dakota featured a host of performance equipment: a Sure-Grip differential, oversized 225/70HR 15 high-speed Goodyear Eagles, and gas shocks. The new Shelby also received styling treatments to set it apart from the standard Dakota.

1990

A new Dakota Club Cab rounded out the Dakota lineup for 1990. It was available in both base and Sport 2WD versions. Built on a 131in wheelbase, the Club Cab added 19in to the cab's length for extra storage space and seating for three additional passengers. A premium version of the Club Cab with split bench seat included four-way adjustable head restraints, driver's side lumbar adjustment, and seat-back storage pockets.

1991

The Dakota Sport convertible and Shelby models did not return for 1991. Carroll Shelby dropped out of the Dodge conversion business to devote his company's time and efforts toward a new Sports Car Club of America racing program. Dodge picked up the ball by putting the optional 5.2L V-8 into the Dakota at the factory. The hood and frame were lengthened 3in to accommodate the V-8.

Dakota models, except the Sport, received a new silver-colored grille with the "Dodge" nameplate now molded into the grille header. Bumpers got a new face bar, and aerodynamic headlights appeared on Sport and L.E. models.

1992

The powerful got more powerful. For 1992, the Dakota turned into a tornado. Major redesigns of the 3.9ltr V-6 and 5.2ltr V-8, as well as significant beefing up of drivelines, made the Dakotas even more appealing. The new Magnum Series engines were available in both 2WD and 4WD models. These engines were not the former engines reworked with bolted-on components, but were new from the bottom up. Dodge claimed they were 80-85 percent new, including multipoint fuel injection.

1993

In appearance and mechanical components, the Dakotas for 1993 were unchanged except for the following items, which made them safer, more comfortable, or more durable: more comfortable bucket seats; a more comfortable premium split bench seat; four-wheel antilock brake system availability; quieter five-speed manual transmission standard with four-cylinder engine; full stainless steel exhaust system; and outboard unibelt restraints with "free running cinching tips."

A 1992 Dakota Club Cab 4WD pickup. This Dakota's front-end style was new for 1991 and remained the same through 1993.

Chapter 13

T300, the New Dodge Ram Pickup

At last, after twenty-two years, Dodge Truck has shot into the future with the introduction of the radical T300 Ram pickup for 1994. It was well worth the wait, as the new Ram transforms truck styling from the routine into the extraordinary.

This dramatic and distinctive new Dodge Ram marks the return of individual personality and character to light-duty trucks. There is absolutely no chance this innovative, world-class pickup will be mistaken for any other truck on the street. Chrysler's award-winning designers made sure of that. They had in mind a truck that would capture the spirit of the original Power Wagon, while at the same time encompassing modern, aerodynamic design cues from such Class 8 big-rigs as Freightliner, Kenworth, and International.

This was the first truck Chrysler developed with its platform team process, bringing better

One of the three new T300s displayed at the "Dodge Ram Pickup World Debut" at Detroit's Cobo Hall on January 5, 1993. This is a 1500 half-ton with the Magnum V-10. It was a special Sport Truck as seen by its painted grille. The V-10 is not intended to be an available option for half-ton trucks. *Paul Kleppert*

products to market faster and more economically. The new Ram was ready in only three years from approval to launch. For a vehicle that's new from the tires up (except for drivelines) and offers an industry exclusive V-10 engine, a thirty-six month cycle was unheard of in the industry. Chrysler would not disclose the Ram's development cost, except to say it was on budget.

As important as style is, it was not the only focus of the new T300. Other vital consideration were functional capabilities and versatility. The new Ram covers all the full-size pickup market segments to accomplish a customer's job better than any other pickup truck in the world. It has the largest standard cab in the industry, along with Club Cabs, and chassis cabs; short and long wheelbases; 2WD and 4WD; five powerful Magnum Series engines—V-6, two V-8s, the V-10, and a new Magnum Cummins Turbo Diesel; three transmissions, and three transfer cases.

Naturally, the T300 is a tough, hard-working truck for hauling and towing, but it also addresses comfort and convenience with innovative features to meet any owner's special needs. The new Ram can be a dynamic rolling office, a quiet place to rest, or just an enjoyable truck to spend leisure time in. Featuring the industry's first 40/20/40 seat, the T300 provides more than adequate room for three people. The center seat back, when folded down, becomes an armrest which can be opened to provide a roomy place to store a cellular phone, fax machine, lap top computer, note pads and pens. This foldaway "business center" was designed for the person who needs a truck to be an office while on the job site or on the highway. Another T300 innovation is the modular storage area behind the seat which includes trays and a nylon net to securely hold tools and other valuables. One other little attention to detail, much appreciated by many drivers, are larger holders for those super-sized soft drink cups.

The new Dodge Ram also provides unequaled safety, with the pickup industry's first standard driver-side air bag, standard two-wheel or optional four-wheel anti-lock braking systems, and side impact beams in the doors.

From now on, Chrysler will market all of its vehicles with a "love-it-or-hate-it" philosophy. No more middle-of-the-road, look alike products from them. Some will shun the new design, but they will be far outnumbered by those who will be compelled to buy a T300. Thanks to the many truck buyers who will satisfy their got-to-have-it urge for a new Ram, Dodge predicts they will triple their full-size pickup sales over the next few years.

Bookcase

The Dodge Story by Thomas A. McPherson. Crestline Publishing, a division of Motorbooks International. Covers all Dodge cars and trucks from 1914 to 1975. Hardbound; 8 1/2 x 11in, 1,500 photographs. Now back in print, this is a valuable volume for the collector.

The Standard Catalog of American Light Duty Trucks 1896-1986 edited by John Gunnell. Krause Publications; available through Motorbooks International. Covers all light-duty trucks built in America from 1896 to 1986. Softcover; 8 1/2 x 11in, 789 pages and 2,000 photographs. Contains prices of collector trucks through 1980 and includes an ID guide, production totals, serial numbers, and specifications. Has a comprehensive Dodge truck section.

The Heavyweight Book of American Light Trucks 1939-1966 by Tom Brownell and Don Bunn with twenty-eight contributing writers. Motorbooks International. Softbound; 8 1/2 x 11in, 528 pages and 715 photos and illustrations. Covers all trucks built in the US from 1939-1966. Has restoration and historical information. It's a regular encyclopedia of light-truck information. Highly recommended.

Dodge Pickups History and Restoration Guide 1918-1971 by Don Bunn and Tom Brownell. Motorbooks International. Softbound, 8 1/2 x 11in, 176 pages and 300 photos and illustrations. A must for the Dodge light-duty truck owner. Contains restoration guides, history of all Dodge trucks, plus clubs and parts sources. Your favorite Dodge truck is covered in detail. Includes everything from double-level panels to Sweptsides.

Pickups and Van Spotter's Guide 1945-1982 by Tad Burness. Motorbooks International. Softbound, 8 1/2 x 9 1/2in, 160 pages and hundreds of illustrations. Its many helpful illustrations cover all Dodge-built pickups and vans; text includes original prices and production figures. A book the collector will find to be very useful as a quick reference resource.

Clubs

American Truck Historical Society
P. O. Box 531168
Birmingham, AL 35253

Antique Truck Club of America
P. O. Box 291
Hershey, PA 17033

Dodge Brothers Club
4451 Wise Rd.
Freeland, MI 48623

This Old Truck
Partick Ertel
P. O. Box 838
Yellow Springs, OH 45387

Military Vehicle Collector's Club
P. O. Box 33697
Thornton, CO 80233

Plymouth Owner's Club
P. O. Box 416
Cavalier, ND 58220

Slant 6 Club of America
P. O. Box 4414
Salem, OR 97302

W. P. C. Club
P. O. Box 3504
Kalamazoo, MI 49003

Suppliers

Automotive Books
Motorbooks International
PO Box 1
Osceola, WI 54020
800-826-6600

Krause Publications
700 E. State St.
Iola, WI 54990

Battery Disconnects
Bathurst, Inc.
PO Box 27
Tyrone, PA 16686

Borg Replacement Clocks
Instrument Services, Inc.
433 S. Arch St.
Janesville, WI 53545

Data Plates
David F. Lodge
Route 1, Box 290B
Saylorsburg, PA 18353

Fenders
Howard Whitelaw
6067 Richmond Ave.
Cleveland, OH 44139

Flat Glass
Glasco
PO Box 276
Tolland, CT 06084

Gauges
Bill's Speedometer Shop
3353 Tawny Leaf
Sidney, OH 45365

Hardware
Restoration Specialities and Supply
PO Box 328, Route 2
Windber, PA 15963

Horns & Electric Wiper Motors
The Horn Shop
7129 Rome-Oriskany Rd.
Rome, NY 13440

Keys & Locks
The Key Shop
144 Crescent Dr.
Akron, OH 44301

Light Lenses
Mike Varosky

1901 Colonia Place #B
Camarillo, CA 93010

Memorabilia
Neil Riddle
452 Newton
Seattle, WA 98109

Original Literature
Dan Kirchner
404 N. Franklin
Dearborn, MI 48128

Jim Lungwitz
PO Box 846
Monticello, MN 55362

Walter Miller
6710 Brooklawn Pkwy.
Syracuse, NY 13211

Robert A. Olds
364 Vinewood Ave.
Tallmadge, OH 44278

Original Parts
Andy Bernbaum
315 Franklin St.
Newton, MA 02158

Arizona Parts
320 E. Pebble Beach
Tempe, AZ 85282

Burchill Antique Parts
4150 24th Ave.
Port Huron, MI 48060

Curtis Equipment Co.
PO Box 506
Raleigh, NC 27602

Dodge City Truck Parts
Route 5
Sunderland, Ontario, Canada
L0C 1H0

John McMahon
6272 Athena
Huntington Beach, CA 92647

Ken Block
PO Box 2459
Cedar Rapids, IA 52406

Len Dawson
1557 Yokeko Dr.
Anacortes, WA 98221

Older Car Parts
3481 S. 152nd St.
Seattle, WA 98188

Roberts Motor Parts
17 Prospect St.
West Newbury, MA 01985

Vintage Power Wagons
Dave Butler
302 S. 7th St.
Fairfield, IA 52556

Pickup Bed Parts
Bruce Horkey Cabinetry
Route 4, Box 188
Windom, MN 56101

Replacement Parts
NAPA Stores
Locations Nationwide

Sun Visor Restoration
Darren DeSantis
67 Lou Ann Dr.
Depew, NY 14043

Tools and Supplies
The Eastwood Co.
580 Lancaster Ave.
Malvern, PA 19355-0296

Vintage Advertisements
Jerry Bougher
3628 Union St.
Albany, OR 97321

Weatherstripping & Mounting Pads
Metro Moulded Parts
PO Box 33130
Minneapolis, MN 55433

Steele Rubber Products
1601 Hwy. 150 E.
Denver, NC 28037

Wiring Harnesses
Rhode Island Wiring Service
PO Box 3737
Peace Dale, RI 02883

YnZ's Yesterdays Parts
333-A E. Stuart Ave.
Redlands, CA 92374

Index